"Satan...You Punk!"

By

Rev. Marvin L. Holden II

© 2002 by Rev. Marvin L. Holden II. All rights reserved.

No part of this book may be reproduced, stored in a retrieval system, or transmitted by any means, electronic, mechanical, photocopying, recording, or otherwise, without written permission from the author.

ISBN: 0-7596-9454-0 (Electronic)
ISBN: 0-7596-9455-9 (Softcover)

This book is printed on acid free paper.

Author's photo by Maurice Merridith

1stBooks – rev. 5/21/02

Dedications

First, and foremost, I dedicate this inspiration to my Lord and Savior Jesus Christ who has kept me through many great trials and tribulations in my life. I thank Him for vision during my blind times and providing a way when all around me was closed. I dedicate this book to my Provider. To my wife, Jill Holden, my strength, my helper and most importantly, my friend. I dedicate this book to you because we know that God is and has always been faithful in our lives. I thank you for gifting me with your undying love. To my blessed daughter, Brittany Alexis, I thank you for giving me reason to live and fight to see you grow into a smart and beautiful woman and allowing me to take part in your nurturing. To my parents, Marvin Sr. and Pearl, I thank you for your love and guidance that has made all of this possible. Also, my sister, Adrienne, who has been my supporter and "cheerleader," I love you. To my in-laws, Catherine and Michael, thank you for believing in me, and especially Catherine for trusting me with your gift, Jill. To my dear friends, Crystal and Chris, thank you for being true friends and supporters throughout. To all of my family, past and present, who have inspired me and believed in my future and have molded my character into the person

I am today. Finally, to those oppressed in sin by the Devil, I dedicate this book to you so that God may come into your life and make it new freeing you from the snares of the enemy.

I am sure the title caught your attention. Christians who have eliminated certain lifestyles and certain language find it difficult or uneasy using the word "punk". Christians have questioned me about calling Satan a punk. Yet, we must understand the real definition of the word. Do you think it is a bit extreme? Should Christians use such terms to make a point? I say yes. Satan is a coward and a hoodlum and in this book you shall see him for who he truly is.

If you feel threatened by the title or calling Satan a punk, I question you. Should Satan receive any glory or profound recognition? Whom do you love, God or Satan? I have no respect for him or shall I even recognize his name worthy of mention.

Look back over your life and examine the problems that Satan has put you, your family, and friends through. Has he riddled your body with diseases and pain? Has he placed your family in financial debt and caused the family to argue about that and other foolishness? Has he made your life full of envy and jealousy? Has he caused someone you love to become depressed and suicidal? Now, I ask you, is he worthy of your kind words or compassion? Not at all! The glory goes to God who can and will deliver you from all tragedy. In this book you will see Satan as an imitator, manipulator, and perpetrator. He is cunning and if you did not know, extremely evil. We will examine his character and his methods. In this book you will recognize his spirit the next time he raises his ugly head and how you can defeat him. Yes, you do have the victory over this "fool" and by the word of God you shall be able to say with boldness, "Satan…You Punk!"

Rev. Holden welcomes your comments, stories, and suggestions at:

Rev. Marvin L. Holden II
P.O. Box 38414
Spanish Lake, MO 63138

IT'S PERSONAL

For so long, all I ever knew was pain. Since the age of two years old, my body has known an invader which science recognizes as Sickle Cell Anemia; however, I know it to be a demon from Hell. This demonic force has tried to eliminate me various times by dropping the oxygen level in my blood to a dangerous point of plaguing me with critical pain. When I was seven years old I was fatally ill and I overheard the doctors tell my parents that I would not live to see my next birthday. Surely, by the grace of God I did; yet, this pain continued to be an active part of my life and so did the statements from doctors regarding me living to a certain age.

Despite having this foe working so hard against me, I continued to live my life and be an active individual. When I entered college the enemy worked his hardest at keeping me out of classes and completing my degrees. I remember a time when my left ankle became infected with leg ulcers. My ankle became swollen, sore, and it was very difficult to walk. Yet, I still limped off to class despite the warnings from my family and girlfriend, (now my wife), Jill. My ankle began to turn toward the left until it literally reached a time that it faced outward. I remember Jill was highly upset with me because I continued on to school, but I told her I could not let this Devil whip me. She understood and knows my determination and the battle I fight each day. I cannot begin to count the many days in which she brought my class work to the hospital. We joke today and say that I received my degrees while lying in the bed of a hospital. Oh yes, I would let nothing stop me.

Once Jill and I married, we began thinking about having children. We felt it was about time because we had been together for seven years (since our high school prom). Here, the Devil raised his ugly head again in our life and had the doctor tell us we could not have children. I remember his words exactly, "Mr. Holden, you could not make the most fertile woman pregnant." I remember laughing when he said that because I recognized the Devil again trying to block our progress.

Sometime afterward, I suffered from depression and suicidal thoughts. It would have been easy for me to commit suicide because I possessed prescribed Demerol pills. The Devil led me to take 33 of these pills while telling a friend on the phone what I was doing. This friend soon called Jill, who raced home and took me to emergency. The doctors and nurses began to feed me a thick, coal-black drink to absorb the medication and induce vomiting. I soon ended up in the psychiatric part of the hospital wondering why I allowed the Devil to get the best of me. My parents helped me through and Jill talked to me and believed in me in order to put me back in place as her husband and friend. I refused to go to any of the support group meetings because I knew what had happened and who had caused my depression...Satan. Also, no one in that support group could offer the support I needed that only God could give. I relied on the Lord even more to bring me out of this depression and self-pity with which Satan was plaguing me. God did just what I asked of Him. After curing the depression, which was a miracle, He performed another that made the statement of the doctor who said Jill could not get pregnant by me out to be a lie. Three months after visiting the doctor, Jill became pregnant. Our daughter, Brittany Alexis-Smith Holden, was born June 15, 1991.

I soon found a job in the field I so desired and for which I had gone to school, journalism. I worked for a newspaper doing everything from hard news to sports (something about which I knew very little). The job was very rewarding with regard to the experience I received and the famous people I met, such as poet laureate Maya Angelou and actress Halle Berry. (No, my wife was not jealous). I enjoyed the work and Satan knew this. So he went back to work activating the anemia and throwing me back into the hospital. He wanted me to lose my job. I soon needed a very serious surgery and I was sure my job was gone and that Satan was going to accomplish what he wanted. However, it did not turn out that way and I kept my job. How embarrassing to know the Lord and still be so full of doubt, however, God still remained Himself even though I did not trust. Yet, I knew Satan had it out for me and for some reason, maybe because I loved the Lord, he had me on his hit list. After all of this I realized that all my past experiences with illness, surgeries, and almost losing my life were just battles. The war with Satan and me was about to begin.

As I went along enjoying my life with my wife and daughter, Satan knew we were happy and he wanted to destroy us. So, in January of 1993, he pulled out his big guns. I had been going to work for a few days noticing some swelling in my left ankle. I thought it was the same problem I suffered before, just an infection. So, I made an appointment with the doctor (no big deal). Days before my doctor's appointment, the swelling increased greatly and moved higher into my leg and the pain became unbearable. I lie on the floor crying in excruciating pain and knew I had to make it to the hospital. When I arrived I was quickly admitted and rushed to a floor. This admission was strange because although I told them I could be suffering from another Sickle Cell Crisis, the doctors believed it to be something else. I really did not begin to worry because I thought nothing could be any worse than what I have already experienced. After much blood work my doctor came into the room and told my wife and me that I had Renal Disease. I asked, "What is that?" He said it is kidney failure. He went on to explain how they had shut down and were not functioning at all. Soon after, more "good" news arrived by way of another doctor, a renal specialist. By now, my mother had arrived and the doctor came in and told us, frankly, that he could not see me living to see the next morning because I had at least 30 pounds of poison running throughout my system. I could see the terror in my mother and Jill's eyes. They did not want to break down and start crying in front of me so they tried to encourage me before easing out of the room. I knew they were crying and scared and it was then that I knew Satan had pulled out his big guns. I began to worry.

Finally, after getting the catheter surgically inserted, I had become very fearful of the dialysis machines because I would suffer from cramping, clotting or infection in my catheter, or I would have a Sickle Cell Crisis. The machine was not my friend and I knew it. I spent the majority of my time crying and singing some spiritual while hooked to this "blood-sucker". I would stare at the machine watching it intensely to make sure it would not take my life, as if there was anything I could do to prevent it. So, I usually prayed for the entire three hours I spent on the machine. My prayer usually went something like, "Lord, don't let this machine kill me. I don't want to die on this machine. I want to live to be with my wife and to raise my daughter. Lord, please." I found myself begging and

The doctor immediately put me on a hemodialysis machine to cleanse my bloodstream of all the poisonous toxins flowing in my body. A doctor came into my room to place a large catheter in my chest next to my left shoulder. The pain was beyond agonizing. I remember the tears pouring down my face due to the pain I felt. Yet, the anger in me toward Satan was too great that I could only express myself with tears. I was so angry that if Satan had been in the physical, he would have been in a grave. While the doctor pierced into my chest with this giant needle, I lie there and cried and thought to myself, "Here we go again. I can never seem to get ahead because of this fool blocking everything that I do. God, I'm tired." This statement had become my anthem, "God, I'm tired."

pleading with tears streaming down my face during all of my treatments. My nurses were very sensitive toward me because they knew I was terrified of the machines and always cried during my treatments.

For the next three months I continued with the hemodialysis until the doctors felt another form of treatment would be gentler to my body. They introduced me to peritoneal dialysis, which involved the surgical implantation of another catheter—this one into my abdomen. This procedure left me as ill as the first. I vomited at least five to six times a day and became seriously ill from the smell or mere thought of food. Nothing stayed in my stomach not even water. The peritoneal dialysis allowed me to get my treatments at home, but the supplies ruled our house. The machine I used was massive and took up quite a bit of space in our bedroom. The bags of saline solution filled our basement to the ceiling. I remember that each box in which the solution came, weighed 50 pounds, and I had 33 boxes delivered each month. Jill would have to carry one of these boxes upstairs each night for me to use. Now, Jill is of no size to lift this type of weight. She is fortunate if she weighs 115 pounds wet. I'm saying that she is very thin and not a physically strong woman; however God gave her the strength. Every night this was our routine while trying to care for a rambunctious two-year-old girl. Yes, it was extremely difficult; yet, God saw us through and met all our needs. Even our financial situation fell upon Jill because my job had let me go. Satan was trying his best to strangle us on every side and place hopelessness in our

Satan...You Punk!

home and in our spirit. He wasn't succeeding. Yes, many of our nights were spent crying and praying, "Lord, when will this be over. Make it soon Lord, please, make it soon." At least every night I would awaken Jill to get me a small pail because I was vomiting, connected to the machine, and could not make it to the bathroom.

So, as she was emptying one pail of vomit I was filling another. This had become a routine for us.

Each day I seemed to get worse with no improvement in sight. By June of 1993 the doctors wanted to place me on the national organ list for a kidney, but they knew I did not have that much time to wait. The usual wait for a kidney is a year to a year and a half and that is if I were Caucasian, yet, I am African-American. So, my wait would be two years or more. The doctors asked if I had any family members who would be willing to test to see if they match me and would donate a kidney. That was funny! I could just see my family running to stand in line to be tested to give a kidney. Huh! That wasn't going to happen. However, my mother and my sister tested but they were not a good match because they each carried the Sickle Cell trait. During all of this, I was praying to God to just turn the kidneys back on. I would even command my body to get back into alliance with the way God created it to be. "Now, kidneys you begin to function and filter my system as God created you to do. Satan, release your hold on my body. I command you in the name of Jesus Christ." Yet, little did I know, God had something already in the making.

Outside of my knowing, Jill had been praying to God to prepare her body to give me a kidney. She told the Lord, "If you don't turn his kidneys back on then I want you to prepare me to give him one of mine." No "if," "ands," or "buts" about it, she told the Lord, "You prepare me because this is what I'm going to do." Jill told the doctors to have her tested and they tried to talk her out of it because they felt the chances were too slim to even try. However, her tenacious spirit insisted, and with some reluctance they went ahead and had her tested. I tried to talk her out of doing this because I had surgeries before and I did not want her to have that experience. Also, I was very nervous for her. We discussed this for a long time, but no matter what I said she was going through with it if she was a match. Jill made an appointment to have her blood drawn. On that day we prayed and said to God, "Let Your will be done." The next day the doctor called and said Jill seemed to be a match, but they wanted to do some more test just to be sure. Jill became overwhelmed with joy and I was excited too, but my anxiety intensified. She went for more test, x-rays, ultra-sounds, and others. After all was done, we went to see the doctor who told us that Jill was not only a 98 percent match, but also a better match that if she were my sister. We were awe struck and could not even conceive what God had just done.

Jill's prayer was answered and my chance for a healthier life was now in view. Satan had been defeated again. He thought he crushed our faith and weakened us to the point where we would just give up. No way was that going to happen. (We just received new hope and about to gain new life.) Our God had just pulled out His big guns and blown Satan off the battlefield. Our entire ordeal had been in God's hands all the time and He wanted to do something that would blow the minds of many people. Our doctors were baffled and could not understand how Jill was so close of a match. They began to talk with her to be sure this was something she wanted to do and someone, meaning me, did not coerce her. In fact, she told them it was quite the opposite. She had to convince me that it was her choice and her answered prayer from God. She went on to tell the doctors that she did not want that for our daughter. Jill went on to say that if our daughter were ever to ask her if there was something that she could have done to save her daddy's life she would not want to tell her, "yes but I didn't try." Jill said she wouldn't be able to live with herself. Also, she said, "I love this man and he is my best friend." With this statement of faith and love the doctors were convinced and began to schedule a date for the surgery.

So many people were puzzled and could not believe Jill was a match and that she was about to give me a vital organ. She had a few people and so-called friends come to her and say, "Girl, no man is worth that. You should get some life insurance on him because you're a nice looking lady and you can get another man." Yet, Jill didn't hear them and continued on in her belief. I was so happy and very anxious to feel healthy again. It had been nine months since I felt good. It has been nine months since I even urinated and had strength to walk or even stand for a short period of time. I wanted to know what it felt like to be well again. Yes, I was eager for health, however, I was very angry with Satan for having me and my family go through something so painful. I took it personally because he had now involved my wife in this war for my health. How dare he pull my family into this! He is going to pay for this action and he is not going to get away. I wanted him to know that he will not lay his hands on my wife during this surgery and he will not harm our daughter at any time. He wasn't invited anywhere near the hospital or the operating rooms. He knew this surgery was going to take place on time and be successful with a quick recovery for the both of us. Yes, he was warned!

Our surgery was on September 28, 1993 about 6 o'clock in the morning. All of our immediate family members were there—nervous, yet, trying to be encouraging. I walked over to Jill's room and told her, "I love you," and she said the same. I asked her was she scared or nervous and she said, "I'm not scared but just a little nervous." "That's understandable," I said, "This is a major surgery but we believe God don't we?" She nodded yes and I continued to say, "We know it will be all right because God confirmed this by having your kidney match me." She nodded yes again. We kissed each other and prayed once more thanking God for the success of the surgery already. The nurses came to take us down and prepared us for the operation. After being prepped, we lie side-by-side on our beds laughing and joking with each other. Soon, a team of doctors came for us. We looked at each other and I said, "I'll see you when we wake up." She said, "I'll see you too. I love you."

Four to five hours later I awakened to see my mother standing over me. I asked her how Jill was doing and she laughed and said, "If you two are not just alike, she asked the same question first when she woke up. She's doing just fine. How are you?" I told her that the kidney is working because I can feel a tremendous difference. My mother was excited and knew the kidney was working also because she could see the urine in a bag that was beside the bed that led from me. The surgery was a success and everyone from the medical staff to our families were still in awe. The nurses soon put us in a room together where we could visit with each other and not have them updating us on each other's condition. Jill left the hospital days before I did and was doing extremely well without any complications. I truly owe this woman my life. She is the best friend that I never had. She is my Godsend and soul mate. I know deep in my heart that the gift she gave was truly a move of God in her spirit. Every time I think of what she did for me I think of the scripture in St. John chapter 15 and verse 13 that reads, "GREATER LOVE HATH NO MAN THAN THIS, THAT A MAN LAY DOWN HIS LIFE FOR HIS FRIENDS." Our love is greater and our lives are much simpler because we appreciate everything in our lives. The simple things mean a lot and we don't waste precious time arguing over foolishness. God has given us peace and increased our love and faith in Him and in each other. The relationship we have I am willing to fight for to keep. The new lease on life that God gave me I am willing to fight to keep. The chance I have to see my daughter grow from a cute little girl into a beautiful and intelligent woman I will fight to keep.

My love for God and my service to Him Satan cannot have. For these reasons and more, I say to Satan, "THIS IS PERSONAL."

IN THE BEGINNING...

The world as we know it today is not the same world that God created or intended. An Earth perfect and absent of sin was the ideal. However, our world is far from perfect and very full of sin. Turn on the television and watch the news. There you will see the anger, hate, famine, and selfishness the world now holds. Where did all of this come from? If God is perfect why isn't the world perfect?

Well, God is perfect and excellent and anything God does is going to be done in that fashion. The Earth was intended for perfect peace and harmony, yielding nourishment for man continuously. All of the Earth was created to glorify, magnify and speak of His excellence. Man was to live in leisure emulating and praising God. He too was to multiply the Earth. A life free from what we know it to be today. A life so rich and abundant that it would surpass understanding. Total tranquillity...but what happened to God's perfect creation?

When God created the heavens it means the entire universe. Also, He created His angelic alliances, which included Lucifer. Yes, God created Lucifer. He is a creation of the Creator. Open your Bible to Genesis 1:1, *"In the beginning God..."* see God was before all.

Next, the Word reads "created". *"God created."* He created the heavens and the Earth.

However, something happens in the very next verse of the first chapter of Genesis.

"The Earth was without form, and void..." Gen. 1:2

The Hebrew words for "without form, and void" are "*tohuw*" and "*bohuw*". Translated into English they mean chaotic, in confusion, waste and empty.

Now the believers of God know that His word reads in First Corinthians 14:33 that *"God is not the author of confusion."* Yet, God is the author of peace and of order and law.

So, something catastrophic happened between verses one and two of Genesis chapter one. There must have been some type of horrifying destruction to take place to cause the entire earth to fall into destruction to take place to cause the entire Earth to fall into total obliteration. Why would He create the Earth in disorder and then have to straighten it out? Does that make sense? The Hebrew word for "created" is "bara", used in Genesis 1:1, implies a perfect and beautiful order and system.

The book of Job shows God communicating with Job about the creation. God asked Job, *"where wast thou when I laid the foundations of the Earth?"* Job was righteous and somewhat proud of his accomplishments. God was whittling him down to humility by a comparison of accomplishments.

God continues, *"who hath laid the measures thereof, if thou knowest? or who hath stretched the line upon it? Whereupon are the foundations thereof fastened [margin, "sunk"]? Or who laid the corner stone thereof; when the morning stars sang together, and all the sons of God shouted for joy?"* Job 38:4-7.

The "morning stars" are light- (truth-) bringing angels and archangels, according to biblical interpretation of symbols. As creations of God, they also are referred to as "all the sons of God." So this, too, implies a perfect and glorious creation of the Earth.

Notice Isaiah 45:18. *"Thus saith the Lord that created the heavens; God Himself that formed the Earth and made it; He hath established it, He created it not in vain."* "In vain" may not be the appropriate translation but rather "waste".

The original Hebrew word there is "tohuw". This Hebrew word is the identical word used in Genesis 1:2, meaning "confusion," or "emptiness," or "waste" — a result of disorder, a result of violation of law. In Isaiah 45:18 we have the plain statement that God created the Earth **NOT** tohuw, that is, not in confusion, not in disorder. Yet, in Genesis 1:2, the Earth was (because it had become) chaotic and in confusion!

So, where did the chaos come from? What sin could have annihilated the Earth and brought it into a condition of void and darkness?

Well, my brother and sister, this sin that caused physical destruction to the Earth was not caused by humanity. The main reason is because no human existed on earth until the sixth day of the re-creation or re-making. We find in I Corinthians 15:45 that Adam is called the first man on this Earth. In Genesis, Eve is called the mother of all living human beings. There was no other race of modern humans prior to Adam and Eve. So, man did not cause this sin that was brought to the Earth.

However, life must have populated the Earth because a sin had occurred on the Earth that brought it into a condition of chaos and confusion by breaking the laws of God. What kind of life populated the Earth prior to Adam and prior to "creation week"?

Notice II Peter 2:4-6. *"For if God spared not the angles that sinned..."* what is this? Angels sinning! *"[v.5] And spared not the old world, but saved Noah the eighth person, a preacher of righteousness, bringing in the flood upon the world of the ungodly; And turning the cities of Sodom and Gomorrah into ashes [God] condemned them with an overthrow, making them an ensample unto those that after should live ungodly."*

Here it mentions the sins from Adam to Noah, and it mentions the physical destruction to the earth as a result of the flood, which was brought about because of the sins of men. Was there a destructive condition brought about on the earth as a result of the "sins of angels"?

The sin of the angels is mentioned first, and it occurred first! There was a devil already there in existence by the time Adam was created. So the sin of the angels happened before the creation of man. Now, remember God gave the angels free will or a choice to serve Him just as He gives humanity that opportunity. If it were not for that this lack of choice would be known as slavery. God does not want to force anyone to serve Him neither does He have too.

The Earth suffered physical destruction as a result of the sins of men. So why would not destruction come upon the Earth as a result of the sins of the angels prior to Adam? Well, you might be asking yourself, "if God is perfect and He creates in perfection, why weren't the angels perfect and free from sin"? How did they obtain their dominion? How did they acquire their power? How did they maintain their control? Where did the Devil get the power to control and to lead and to rule this world?

We will examine the fall of Satan and his allies and how the world is under subjection to these fallen angels. You will learn why Satan is wreaking havoc with your life, family, home, community, school, work, and all of society. You will be upset with the spirit of evil that hovers over our souls and creates animosity between us all. Your eyes will be opened to the nature of the sin and not the character of the sinner. The anger, bitterness, and hatred you may carry for the liar will be moved from them to the "father of lies". You will be able to fight off the temptations of the devil because you will finally understand who he is and how he operates. Sin will become a vile taste in your mouth and in your life. You will be the bold and strong Christian to tear down strongholds against you and the ones you love. My friend, you will regain the peace that Satan has stolen from you. You will be victorious in the Holy Spirit once you grasp the tricks of Satan. Then you will be ready to stand steadfast, and unmoveable and shout aloud for the entire world to hear, "Satan…You Punk!"

LUCIFER — HOW ART THOU FALLEN FROM HEAVEN?

Let us investigate the origin of Satan and find out how he landed the title of the Evil One.

In the 28th chapter in the book of Ezekiel verses 11-19, God reveals the lamentation (mourning or grieving) for the angelic king of Tyre: Satan. Now, all that is said of the king of Tyre here must be understood as having a double reference- to the earthly king of Tyre, a man, but also, to the supernatural king, Satan or Lucifer, who ruled Tyre through the earthly monarch. Both the earthly and supernatural kings are referred to and addressed in this prophecy. Statements that could refer to the human being must be understood as concerning him [King of Tyre]; and those that could not be spoken of a man must be recognized as referring to the supernatural being [Lucifer].

The meaning of double reference — when a visible creature is addressed but certain statements also refer to an invisible person who is using the visible creature as a tool. A good and simple example is the case of Christ addressing Peter as Satan. When Peter declared that he would never permit anyone to crucify his Lord on the cross, Christ rebuked him saying, *"Get thee behind Me Satan: thou art an offence unto Me: for thou savourest not the things that be of God, but those that be of men"* (Mt. 16:22-23). Both Satan and Peter are addressed in the same statement, and both are involved in the rebuke. Peter, for the moment, was unknowingly used as a tool of Satan in an effort to keep Christ from going to the cross. Primarily, Satan was the one addressed; and so it is with the passage above, where a visible creature is addressed, and the primary reference is to an invisible being. This is the double reference we find in Ezekiel.

The earthly king in verse 12 is Ithobalus II and the supernatural king is undoubtedly Lucifer, who is mostly referred to in this prophecy. The passage goes on to say, *"thou sealest up the sum, full of wisdom, and perfect in beauty."* Let us understand this passage of scripture..."thou sealest up the sum," means Lucifer was created complete, finished, and a perfect pattern created by God.

Lucifer was given "full wisdom" which is still true of him and which could not be true of any earthly king of Tyre. With all of those qualities: finished, perfect, and full of wisdom, these are the characteristics of Lucifer that lead to his downfall. Along with "perfect beauty", which does not apply to any fallen man, caused Lucifer's pride and fall.

Lucifer had charge over Eden, the Garden of God, and verse 13 tells us how beautifully it is adorned. Precious stones of jasper, sapphires, diamond, emeralds, and gold is the foundation of the kingdom and his throne. Now my friend, with all of this in mind, can you see how this could have gone to his head. Most people could not handle just one of these gifts alone. Many times we find it difficult to be around individuals who believe they are beautiful and are extremely vain. People who are unaccustomed to good and precious gifts act as so. This grandiose behavior we see developing in Lucifer.

In verse 15 we find the reason for Lucifer's fall. His vanity became his wickedness and his heart became lifted.

"Thou wast perfect in thy ways from the day that thou wast created, till iniquity (great wickedness or injustice) was found in thee...thine heart was lifted up because of thy beauty...[v.18] thou hast defiled thy sanctuary by the multitude of thine iniquities...[v.19] all they that know thee among the people shall be astonished at thee: thou shalt be a terror, and never shalt thou be any more."

He has ruined his own domain and his own being believing he is the best creation that God created. Lucifer placed himself above everything. He thought he was better than all that was created. For that reason, he defiled everything around him and was brought down from his governorship of the Earth and God's garden. He is now a terror and a nightmare to humanity.

However, there was a relationship between Lucifer and God that had to be remarkable for God to ornate such a place for Lucifer. The bible tells us how beautiful the Earth was before Adam, so it must go with out saying that God also fashioned the habitats of the other angels similar. Lucifer is created perfect in beauty and his ways. So, why give all of this up? Could this be part of God's mysterious plan to throw Lucifer into pride? Or, is it just Lucifer's own freedom of choice to become grandiose that places him in an evil position?

In the book of Isaiah chapter 14 verse 12-14 shows us the imitating character of Lucifer and how he plans to take over the heavens.

"How art thou fallen from heaven, O Lucifer, son of the morning! How art thou cut down to the ground, which didst weaken the nations! For thou hast said in thine heart, I will ascend into heaven, I will exalt my throne above the stars of God: I will sit also upon the mount of the congregation, in the sides of the north: I will ascend above the heights of the clouds; I will be like the most High."

How shameless is Lucifer? He is not shameless at all. Here he has the nerve, the guile, and the audacity to say, "I will be like the most High." This is utterly foolish and diabolical. In this plan to overtake the heavens Lucifer devised a way to lead one-third of the angels into open rebellion against God.

In the book of Jude chapter one verse six we see the angels leaving their God-given domains and following Lucifer into his punishment and sentence.

"And the angels which kept not their first estate, but left their own habitation, he hath reserved in everlasting chains under darkness unto the judgment of the great day."

Angels leaving the heavens to go into total darkness is absurd. God placed Lucifer and all of the angels in excellence and they turned their backs on God's law and gave it all away. What could have Lucifer told them to make them give all of that away? What sweet words could he have whispered in their ears? How cunning could he be? Rest assure, whatever he said it was a lie!

Now with all the evil in his heart and his ill-prepared masterplan to war for the right to govern heaven, he is marked as the Evil One or the great dragon, as Revelation 12:4, 7-9 states.

"...And there was war in heaven: Michael and his angels fought against the dragon; and the dragon fought and his angels, and prevailed not; neither was their place found any more in heaven. And the great dragon was cast out, the old serpent called the Devil, and Satan, which deceiveth the whole world: he was cast into the Earth, and his angels were cast out with him."

Satan and his fallen angels [demons] are here on the Earth to do just as the scripture states, "deceive the whole world." My friend, I tell you that our foes are bitter and full of hate at losing their place in heaven. They have no one else to blame but themselves; however, you and I will be the ones to suffer their frustrations.

So, in order to deceive Christians, Satan and his cohorts must appear to us as Christ-like. He will imitate Christ by name and by character to fool and lead us away from the true Lord and Savior Jesus Christ.

Remember that the prophet Isaiah told us in Chapter 14 of Satan's pride and mocking spirit. Well, in verse 12 the name Lucifer means light-bringer [Latin], daystar, and son of the morning in Hebrew. Well, you may be asking, "why is this significant?" It is important that Christians reveal Satan and not mistake him for Christ. Let me show you. Lucifer or light-bringer is the equivalent of the Greek word, "Phosphorous," meaning luminescence, which is used as a title of Christ in II Peter

1:19 [daystar]. This corresponds to the name "radiant and brilliant Morning Star" in Revelation 22:16, a name Jesus called Himself. Satan will cause us to believe he is Christ by saying the right words and making his actions appear Christ-like. All of those antics are just to fool believers and unbelievers to follow him.

In the book of Ezekiel chapter 28 verse 14 God says to Lucifer, *"you were the anointed cherub"*. Meaning, God created him to be a select or special angel but he failed in that position. We know Lucifer failed because the scripture reads, "you were anointed...," meaning he did not live up to his place in God. Lucifer failed God by allowing the "special" quality to go to his head.

Satan has now stepped well beyond his boundaries with regard to God's law. He has become an ugly spirit for his shear attempt to take over the heavens with a throne God created and gave to him. We are talking about a spirit that is mindless and void of any respect for anyone. Yet, this gutless coward thought it could be done. He persuaded his cohorts and filled their spirit with slander to turn them away from God.

The scriptural proof for these other angelic forces and establishments are in Colossians 1:15-18. The word of God confirms there are thrones, dominion's, principalities, and powers, visible and invisible, created in heaven and in Earth. The scripture shows the establishment of kingdoms in many places in the heavens and other planets other than the Earth.

Well, now Satan and his demons are roaming the Earth filled with bitterness and hatred. Now they are looking for someone to lash out on and mankind is the prey. Let us examine how this happened by beginning in Genesis 1:26,28.

"God said, Let Us [Father, Son, Holy Spirit] make mankind in Our image, after Our likeness, and let them have complete authority over the fish of the sea, the birds of the air, the [tame] beasts, and over all of the Earth, and over everything that creeps upon the Earth (Amp. Bible version)."

In verse 28 the same states that man is now the ruler or governor of the Earth. Meaning that Satan and his allies are subject to man's authority and they know this to be true. He is stripped of his rule and becomes outraged. We also see that Satan or the angels themselves were not created in the image or likeness of God. Resembling God could spark some jealousy and envy. The ideal that mankind is walking the Earth looking and acting like God could be a harsh reminder to this demonic force. So, if they did not want to obey God and His law, they certainly are not going to give us an easy time.

So Satan manages to cleverly trick man out of his God-given position or man's ignorance allowed it as revealed in Genesis 3:1/

"Now the serpent was more subtle [hard to grasp, elusive, acute, ingenious, cunning, clever, and working insidiously] and crafty than any living creature of the field which the Lord God had made. And he [Satan] said to the woman, Can it really be that God has said, You shall not eat from every tree of the garden?"

Satan...You Punk!

Here Satan twists and turns the tables on Eve by letting her decide on this tempting question. Satan weaves his web of deceit by infiltrating humanity via the woman, Eve, who then gave to Adam, causing them both to fall from God-consciousness to self-consciousness.

Adam and Eve lost the power to do good and gained the power to do evil. Therefore, in his cowardice, Satan petitioned the woman. He caused a shy insinuation calculated to excite a natural curiosity. He also used a direct lie combined, however, with just enough truth to give plausibility.

Now, what is this? Man giving up his position in God's paradise on Earth to fall into the darkness of Satan. Sounds familiar? Satan and the angels lost their place in God so now, it is man's turn. Doesn't that sound like a jealous spirit? Yes!!

My friend, understand that Satan's work is to oppose God whenever possible. His great work is to cause the fall of man, usurp his dominion, and prevent the Messiah's coming in order to avert his own defeat and pending doom.

Satan uses every conceivable means to keep mankind subject to him and to keep Christians from serving God. If his attempt fails, he then tries to kill the believer's testimony and ruin his belief in God.

"And these are they by the wayside, where the word is sown, but when they have heard, Satan cometh immediately, and taketh away the word that was sown in their hearts" (St. Mark 4:15).

Satan will try to make a fallen believer or backslider remain fallen or tempt you with thoughts of suicide. He will insist to you that there is no other way out of the torment but hides the fact that self-murder will be the beginning to real torment in eternal Hell. The Devil knows the word of God says in Exodus 20:13 that, *"thou shalt not kill,"* but remember Satan could care less for God's word.

Satan will condition man to be complacent in his attitude for serving God. If he succeeds, he urges men to stay in that condition so that God will cut them off in the end.

"So then because thou art lukewarm, and neither cold nor hot, I will spew thee out of my mouth" (Rev. 3:16).

God can neither use nor trust a wishy-washy individual. If that person, he or she, is unsure about himself or herself it is certain they would not know whom to serve, God or Satan. For that reason God has nothing to do with him or her.

The Devil will also make people think they are missing everything in life if they fail to engage in all kinds of sins, which will damn their souls. Satan places major emphasis on sin and sinful pleasures as innocent fun. He will stir unholy pleasures in men and women causing them to lose all restraint and live life in revelry. Satan's endeavor is to convince people that there is no joy in serving God.

He leads mankind to believe that material items are all that matter in life. Satan whispers to man to be diligent in business and take all of his time to get rich before serving the Lord. However, when a person truly serves the Lord, he will be abundantly blessed over and over.

"Therefore take no thought, saying, what shall we eat? Or, what shall we drink? Or where withal shall we be clothed? [v.33] But seek ye first the kingdom of God, and his righteousness; all these things shall be added unto you" (Mt. 6:31-33).

The word of God tells us to rely on Him and He will supply our needs. His word also tells us to give and by doing that we will be overly blessed.

"Give, and it shall be given unto you; good measure, pressed down, and shaken together, and running over, shall men give into your bosom. For with the same measure that ye mete withal it shall be measured to you again" (Lk. 6:38).

Another strategic tactic of Satan is to encourage church leaders [pastors, apostles, prophets, evangelists, and teachers] to lower and compromise the standards of holy living. These ministers preach "feel good" stories, fables, and current events rather than the unadulterated word of God.

Satan's final method is to cause children and adults to engage in juvenile "punkish" behavior. He dares men to take chances in evil diversions. Satan tempts mankind with drugs and alcohol, lustful people, and stealing and murder. These are indulgences people would not ordinarily commit; yet, they become fooled into those circumstances. He will cause men to challenge one another manhood and bravery by using such words as sissy, momma's boy, or punk. Remember that Satan will always turn the tables on you when he is the true "punk".

THE PUNK

"Punk": [def. Webster] (1) a dry substance that burns slowly without a flame: used esp. to light fireworks, decayed wood. (2) hoodlum; of poor quality; worthless; coward.

You may agree that the first definition could apply to Satan also. His spirit is as decayed wood, which in the end will have the opportunity to burn slowly. Yet, we need to discuss his character. Let us begin with the word "hoodlum" which means gangster, a member of a criminal element; lawless.

When Satan challenged God and broke His law it made him felonious. His ability to lure other angelic powers into his sinister plot discloses his gangster; hoodlum-like character. Yet, his blatant "chicken-hearted" personality proves he does not have the courage to stand up to God on his own. There is strength in numbers and only a fool will stand-alone. However, I believe anytime someone chooses to go against God, alone or in a group, he or she are complete fools!

The Gospel according to St. John 10:10 refers to Satan as a thief, one who steals. Satan wants to steal not only our souls away from God, but also steal the glory and honor from God.

Examine how the thief operates. Satan moves through the shadows of the night, while no one is watching, when the victim least suspect it. However, when confronting the thief, he is subjugating, frightened and extremely nervous of the believer. The fallen angels [demons] fall under this subjugation also. They are so afraid of God and His word that they quiver and flee at the presence of the anointing. An example of this "sissy" behavior is found in St. Matthew 8:28-32.

In these passages of scripture we find devils scared by the very presence of our Lord and Savior Jesus Christ. The scripture tells of two men under the control of demons moving fiercely through a graveyard. Acting through these individuals, these devils were boldly scaring people and showing them how turbulent they are. However, in verse 29 a difference in the demons behavior begins. Their boisterous and bullying behavior becomes nervous. Why? (The presence of the Son of God.) The demons say to Jesus, "art thou come hither to torment us before the time?" Do you see the "punkish" behavior? The demons are frightened war will occur before their final demise. The victory over the Devil and his gang is to come, yet they are so scared they beg Jesus not to suffer [agonize] them. They want to be cast into the herd of hogs where the hogs then drowned themselves. This passage is amazing, inspiring, and victorious. It shows Christians too can tame, control, and overpower this loudmouth "punk".

Also, notice in the previous verse that Jesus refrains from saying a word to these demons. They are trembling at the shear and overwhelming presence of Christ. Yet, when Jesus does speak in verse 32, the only word He says is, "Go". Hallelujah, hallelujah, just one small word and these "fools" take off running.

We as Christians have this power. In the book of James chapter 4 verse 7 reads, *"submit yourselves therefore to God. Resist the devil, and he will **flee from you."*** By submitting ourselves to the will of God He gives us the anointing, authority, and jurisdiction above Satan and his bumbling troops. To resist the Devil means not to fall for his tempting bait. Be vocal in your resistance to Satan and tell him aloud that he has no authority in your life. Feed him with the word of God because that is our promise. Satan does not want to hear the promises of God.

However, you throw it at him every chance you get and do not stop rebuking him daily. Our battle with him is daily and we must stay in constant prayer to heed the commands of God on how to slaughter those demonic forces. With that type of power, the believer should have a sense of excitement and joy. Ask any war veteran or survivor about the feeling they had when they learned the war was over. I am sure they will inform you of the joy and liberty that filled the air. God gives us that emotion when we are victorious over Satan and his temptations. Then we can stand over Satan in his agony and his failed attempt to over take us and say to him, "Satan…you punk!"

He infiltrates the human spirit and manifests his evil spirit and lust into the hearts of mankind. Satan's greatest and most important work is to con men with his pseudo-reign, pseudo-power, and his pseudo-authority. He conceals himself and deceives men with false doctrine and experiences with God as stated in 2 Cor. 11:14-15.

"And it is no wonder, for Satan himself masquerades [a false show for pretense or concealment of the truth] as an angel of light; so it is not surprising if his servants also masquerade as ministers of righteousness. [But] their end will correspond with their deeds" (Amp. Bible).

Ministers masquerading are the problem that plagues many churches. Their insincerity to the Gospel of Jesus Christ leads many people away from the church and scares others from believing the true servants of God.

Satan will also cause Christians to turn from their faith and begin to believe the double-dealing. We have Christians calling the telephone psychic-lines trying to find an answer instead of praying to God for the miracle. There are those who are finding themselves into new age religions and "channeling" and not seeking the power of the Holy Spirit who will give them clarity.

"But the [Holy} Spirit distinctly and expressly declares that in latter times some will turn away from the faith, giving attention to deluding and seducing spirits and doctrines that demons teach.

Through the hypocrisy and pretensions of liars whose consciences are seared [cauterized]" (1 Tim. 4:1-2, Amp. Bible).

By turning away from the Holy Spirit and giving your attention to "seducing spirits," the believer's mind becomes destroyed. Soon after, the believer is affixed on lies and begins to crave nothing else.

Satan…You Punk!

It is certain that every religion or doctrine among mankind is not of God. We must examine and seek knowledge through the plain written word of God as 1 John chapter 4 verse 1 states.

"Beloved, believe not every spirit, but try the spirits whether they are of God: because many false prophets are gone out into the world." (KJV).

This passage simply informs the Christian not to fall for everyone or anything. There are a lot of people selling "snake oil" so we must challenge the seller to prove to us that his oil is anointed. Yet, Satan will invoke fear or embarrassment into your spirit so that you won't challenge him but, be bold and stand on the word of God. If it is of God you will know and if it is not, you will know. The point is to be in the realm of knowledge and not to be ignorant of anything.

The knowledge of the truth is the first key to a winning warfare against devils and untruth. The first clause of Hosea 4:6 says, *"my people are destroyed for lack of knowledge:"*

Christians do not let your guards down and end up outside the knowledge of God. We must know God's word and be able to recognize His Spirit. Take time out of your busy day and commune with the Lord and ask Him to make His spirit familiar to you. So, when the Lord does present Himself to you, you will know and not be oblivious or ashamed.

Sometimes we find ourselves as dear trapped in the headlights of an oncoming speeding car when we, as believers, accept anything and everything as "divine" inspiration or revelation from God.

Remember that we are very appetizing prey when we become believers in Christ. However, being a believer will not stop him [Satan] from trying to pass himself off to Christians as God. We are the ones whom he is against.

When we allow Satan to let us neglect the word of God, we fall prey to one or many of his demons. They will whisper to our spirit saying, "don't waste a beautiful day reading the Holy Bible. Go out and enjoy yourself…read it next time." Realize ignorance will not be your wall of protection against the enemy. Resist that spirit of procrastination and laziness. Exercise your faith and the word of God every moment you get. When you do that you are allowing the Holy Spirit to come and minister to you and lead you into happiness. Romans 10:3 lets us know we must submit ourselves to God.

"For they being ignorant of God's righteousness, and going about to establish their own righteousness, have not submitted themselves unto the righteousness of God."

We are out of our minds when we start saying, "I can do this on my own." Yes, my Christian friend, we need God's righteousness and knowledge as our refuge. As wise Christians, we should be educated, calculated, and alert to the tactics of this scoundrel [Satan]. He can take an individual and have them to rest in their beliefs and interpretation of the Holy Bible without seeking God's meaning. That is how we can fall out of God's righteousness and into our own ignorant righteousness.

By studying and communing with the Lord, he makes us wise to the snares and tricks of the Devil. God makes us strong and more like Him the more we study Him.

"Lest Satan should get an advantage of us: for we are not ignorant of his devices" (2 Cor. 2:11).

Ignorance is a tool of Satan's and he uses it to control the hearts of men. Ignorance accounts for his widespread success in persuading men to accept the suggestions of false doctrines, ideas, leadings, and guidance. Satan wants us complacent and inactive when it comes to studying and living the word of God. Once he [Satan] has us in that position, we are vulnerable to him and his forces.

Any doctrine that denies or causes disbelief concerning Kingdom principles taught in the scripture is from Satan and his demons.

"But refuse and avoid irreverent legends (profane and impure and godless fictions, mere grandmother's tales) and silly myths, and express your disapproval of them. Train yourself toward godliness (piety), [keeping yourself spiritually fit]." (1 Tim. 4:7 Amp. Bible)

Do not let Satan rear his ugly head. When you hear "sugar-coated" teaching, stand on your principles and censor such nonsense. We must hold steadfast to the Gospel plow. The scripture reads, "train yourself toward godliness". For so long we have done evil that we are conditioned to believing that is all we can do. This is another trick of the Devil. We can become godly people. All we must do is align ourselves with God and learn. I read a story sometime ago about Scottie Pippen of the Chicago Bulls basketball team. In the story he talked about being envious of his fellow teammate, Michael Jordan and how he seemed to have fallen in his game because of this. He soon realized that he could sit and be bitter or get up off his butt and train with Jordan and become better. No need to say he chose the latter. This is what we as believers in Christ must do and that is to get up off our butts and our "coulda, shoulda, and wouldas" and train with God. Keep exercising to strengthen your faith and you will be immune to the Devil's foolish doctrines.

Satan will cause man to create religions and doctrine to deny the true inspiration of the virgin birth and the divinity of Christ. He continues to cause disbelief of Christ's miraculous power, ministry, death, burial, and bodily resurrection and ascension into heaven. He will also lead Christians to believe that Jesus Christ will not come again and He has not set up an eternal kingdom.

"And every spirit that confessth not that Jesus Christ is come in the flesh is not of God: and this is that spirit of [the] antichrist, whereof ye have heard that it should come; and even now already is it in the world." (1 John 4:3)

Satan, to this day, is still telling the world that there is no Christ. So why are Christians waiting for His return?

Remember Satan's character. He is the father of lies and a murderer (Jn. 8:44), he is cunning, and the first sinner and rebel. He, himself, is filled with self-gratification and goes against all society.

How does Satan work his wickedness through mankind and how can we recognize it? Well, as I previously stated, he uses ignorance and deception. We must guard ourselves against these qualities. The Devil extensively exercised the power of death until Christ conquered death, hell, and the grave.

"Forasmuch then as the children are partakers of flesh and blood, he also himself likewise took part of the same; that through death he might destroy him that had the power of death, that is, the devil" (Heb. 4:14).

Because Christ came as a man, died, and rose defeating Satan's power, we too are partakers in that victory.

Yet, the victory in Christ, we as believers can stand over Satan and yell, *"O death, where is thy sting? O grave, where is thy victory?" (1 Cor. 15:55).*

Satan has to get it through his thickhead that he has no hold on us.

However, Satan has people who will follow him and are committed to his ways. He is the leader of all sinners and backsliders as 1 John 3:8-10 informs us.

"He that committeth sin is of the devil; for the devil sinneth from the beginning. For this purpose the Son of God was manifested, that he might destroy the works of the devil. Whosoever is born of God doth not commit sin; for his seed remaineth in him: and he cannot sin, because he is born of God. In this the children of God are manifest, and the children of the devil: whosoever doeth not righteousness is not of god, neither he that loveth not his brother."

When you live a sinful life you belong to the Devil and he is your father. The sinner does not belong to God because he does not love his brother [fellow man] or God, but God loves him. Yet, Christ came to release us from the bondage of this sinister character.

Another employment of Satan is physical, and mental maladies throughout the world. He uses diseases as a weapon to prohibit man from successfully doing the will of God. Illness, which taxes people's God-given health, causes man to doubt the healing power of God.

"How God anointed Jesus of Nazareth with the Holy Ghost and with power: who went about doing good, and healing all that were oppressed of the devil; for God was with him" (Acts 10:38).

Through the blood of Jesus Christ we have this power and anointing to heal. God's word tells us that we can do greater than He can. The evidence for this is found in St. John 14:12.

"Verily, verily, I say unto you, he that believeth on Me, the works that I do shall he do also; and greater works than these shall he do; because I go unto my Father."

Imagine doing greater works than Christ does. Is that possible? Of course, with Christ all things are possible. We just need to yield to His grace and He will make the impossible, possible. Further proof of Christ's healing power over Satan's rule of sickness is found in the gospel according to St. Luke 13:11, 16 in which Jesus heals a handicapped woman.

"And there was a woman there who for eighteen years had an infirmity caused by a spirit [a demon of sickness]. She was bent completely forward and utterly unable to straighten herself up or to look upward. [v.16] *and ought not this woman, a daughter of Abraham, whom Satan has kept bound for eighteen years, be loosed from this bond on the Sabbath day?"* (Amp. Bible).

My friend, you may be bound by an infirmity that Satan has kept you in for years, but trust me the power of Christ will come and destroy the yoke. Satan will whisper to you and have you depressed and feeling alone and that no one cares. I say to you, do not fret, God cares and loves you. He will break the tie that binds and release all worry and doubt. However, you must relax in the Spirit of God because He is giving you the strength to endure. Just as He is strengthening you He will heal you. Do not let Satan play mind games with you.

Another field that Satan masters is temptation or the lure. Christians and sinners fall in this trap just as they would with a good con-artist or street hustler. Satan even had the nerve to tempt Jesus.

"And He was there in the wilderness forty days, tempted of Satan; and was with the wild beasts; and the angels ministered unto Him." (Mk. 1:13).

So if Jesus, our Lord and Savior, can be tempted by Satan, who are we not to be tried by him?

So, if this "fool" had the guile to try Jesus the Christ, who are we? We fall very short in the grace and Excellency of our Lord and Savior. We need the tremendous strength and intelligence granted only through Jesus Christ.

Satan will try and overtake us through the works of the flesh as told in Galatians 5:19.

"Now the works of the flesh are manifest, which are these; Adultery, fornication, uncleanness, lasciviousness..."

The cowardly behavior of adultery and fornication consist of lying and deceiving. Adulterers lie to their spouse of their whereabouts and sneak to make time for their adulterous act. Satan lies to their minds and makes them feel comfortable with their acts by calling them ["affairs," "flings," "lovers," or even "their just a friend"]. Yet, the word of God tells us in 1 Corinthians 7:1-5 how to resist the Devil's wiles.

"...It is well [advantageous, expedient, profitable, and wholesome] for a man not to touch a woman [to cohabit with her] but to remain unmarried. But because of the temptation to impurity and to avoid immorality, let each [man] have his own wife and let each [woman] have her own husband. For the wife does not have [exclusive] authority and control over her own body, but the husband [has his rights]; likewise also the husband does not have [exclusive] authority and control over his body, but the wife [has her rights].

Do not refuse and deprive and defraud each other [of your due marital rights], except perhaps by mutual consent for a time, so that you may devote yourselves unhindered to prayer. But afterwards resume marital relations, lest Satan tempt you [to sin] through your lack of restraint of sexual desire."(Amp. bible).

I believe this is the measure we have to take to prevent Satan from trapping us. By keeping our interest and affections focused on our spouses Satan loses. Don't allow yourself to view this passage of scripture as being sexist. We all know that in marriage it takes a considerable amount of work to keep it going and for both parties to be happy. Let Satan's foolishness go when it comes to your marriage. Don't sit around arguing about sex. Let the word of God be your guide to your marital relations. Don't let Satan lure you away with the sweet fragrance and beautiful physique of another woman; the charming, gentlemanly, and muscular built of another man. Find those and the other alluring qualities in your mate that made you first fall in love. When married couples exercise this passage of scripture, no devil in Hell will be able to find a wedge in your marriage.

What about those individuals who are single, how do they live holy before God? Those who dabble or lose themselves in fornication use deceptive tactics too. In most relationships, men and women find themselves lying to each other just to get to the point...sex. Many of the lies are "yes, baby I love you," "I'll do anything for you," "you know I'm the only one for you," and "I'm totally yours".

Young people who entertain themselves in fornication have to sneak around the schedules of their parents or guardians. These lies lead to feelings being deeply hurt and wounded. Lies and fornication will escort you into a hopeless tragedy, such as, a child born out of wedlock; many times fatherless or motherless. The lies and wild emotions can cause a couple or lady to contemplate abortion [murder]. My friend, guard yourselves from the "dead-end" and irresponsible life that Satan wants to provide for you.

Sexual abstinence is a term that Satan has coined in the hearts of mankind as a joke. Many people will indulge in fornication believing if they don't, something must be "wrong" with them. Satan will make your peers call you a freak, homosexual, or a punk.

You must recognize how Satan will turn the tables on you. In 1 Thessalonians 4:3-5 is about abstaining from sex.

"For this is the will of God, that you should be consecrated [separated and set apart for pure and holy living]: that you should abstain and shrink from all sexual vices. That each one of you should know how to possess [control, manage] his own body in consecration [purity, separated from things profane] and honor. Not [to be used] in the passion of lust like the heathen, who are ignorant of the true God and have no knowledge of His will." (Amp. Bible).

God has a higher purpose for our lives than for it to be shamelessly used in unholy living. He wants the Christian and the unbeliever to abandon the lustful wiles of Satan. You may say, "that's easier said than done". Well, that may be true, however, God has given man the power to "control" his body. That control comes from the knowledge [fear] of God, which will keep you in His, will [law].

With respect to keeping God's will, we, Christians, are mindful of how we present ourselves to the Lord. Our presentation to the Lord must be attractive and void of any sinful stain. The Apostle Paul wrote in Romans 12:1

"...*that ye present your bodies a living sacrifice, holy, acceptable unto God, which is your reasonable service.*" Single people must understand that they are not exempt from this service to God. When dating, couples must hold true to the laws of God and resist temptation whether you are together seven minutes, seven hours, seven days, or with a seven years itch. Your body is a temple of God created by God, and Satan wants to reside in and then destroy that temple of God. God instituted marriage, "*therefore shall a man leave his father and his mother, and shall cleave unto his wife; and they shall be one flesh*" (Gen. 2:24). However, Satan does not honor marriage and he teaches mankind not to honor it.

Galatians 5:19-21 further tells us of the workings of Satan through the flesh. The letter of the Apostle Paul to the Galatians lists uncleanness, hatred, wrath, envying, lasciviousness, murder, drunkenness, etc. If you examine all of these wiles, you can recognize the cowardice and spiritless qualities in them. It is a quality totally parallel to Satan and being partakers of Satan's foolish sport, you "...shall not inherit the kingdom of God". My friend, you need to awaken yourself to the desperation, irresponsibility, and ignorance evident throughout this passage of scripture.

The Evil One will also try to marvel us with false miracles and lying astonishment as written in 2 Thessalonians 2:9.

"*The coming [of the lawless one, the antichrist] is through the activity and working of Satan and will be attended by great power and with all sorts of [pretended] miracles and signs and delusive marvels — [all of them] lying wonder"* (Amp. Bible).

He will set traps and snares for men to fall if they are not in good standing. Good standing, meaning "LIVING" God's word everyday and not just when it is time to go to church. In Paul's first epistle to Timothy, chapter 3 verse 7, we are told to be upstanding Christians lest we fall in the devil's pit.

"Furthermore, he must have a good reputation and be well thought of by outside [the church], lest he become involved in slander and incur reproach and fall into the devil's trap" (Amp. Bible).

Satan will hinder prayer, cause diversion, and blind men to the Gospel as found in [2 Cor. 4:4]. Satan will cause wavering and unstableness as found in [James 1:5-8].

"If any of you lack wisdom, let him ask of God, that giveth to all men liberally, and upbraideth not; and it shall be given him. But let him ask in faith, nothing wavering. For he that waverth is like a wave of the sea driven with the wind and tossed. For let not that man think that he shall receive any thing of the Lord. A double minded man is unstable in all his ways."

Satan can take the smallest spark of doubt that is in your heart or mind and turn it into your hardest mountain to climb. You, as a believer in Christ, must be filled with total undaunted faith. If Satan detects any fear in you he will cause you to feel unsure of your prayer and your place in God.

Satan, furthermore, causes darkness, oppression, deadness, and weakness. Men and women have procrastinated and compromised their belief and ministry because of the intimidation Satan has placed in their hearts. Christians have put off God-given callings and orders in fear of what people [believers and unbelievers] will think. These Christians will also give in to the will of the Evil One and his workers.

The Christian then finds himself giving the right of way to the enemy instead of to the will of God. Yet, we must be serious because, *"...your adversary the devil, as a roaring lion, walketh about seeking whom he may devour."* (1 Peter 5:8).

If we are not careful and observant we will be consumed. Satan will hide in the tall grass [shadows] waiting for the opportune time to begin his hunt. He waits for you to fall prey by his threats and then he consumes us.

These are his qualities and the way he operates. In the natural he appears to Christians as the thief who enters our home and steals everything in sight. He is the crazed "fool" who snatches children off the street, molesting and killing them. He is the leader of the church who tickles the ears with emotion instead of the sincere word of God. He is the one who leaves a mother crying in the street over her son's dead body. He is the spouse who creeps home late and eases into the bed without any explanation. He is the disobedient child at home and school. He is the drug dealer who settles in the bowels of the ghetto and the one who lives lavishly in high society corporate America. He is the rapist who gloats in his selfishness after committing a violent act. He is the one who riddles a healthy body with disease, tumors, and infection. Oh yes, he is the culprit behind all wickedness and evil. He is the one who fills your heart with greed and leads you to believe that God will send you a credit card with an 18 percent interest-rate and then lead you into financial debt. He is the head of corrupt government who leads nations into war and civil unrest. He has stripped nations barren and caused famine and desolation. He is the master of heterosexual divorce and the architect of homosexual marriages. Look at the confusion he stirs up in the hearts of mankind. It is not a wonder we are banging our heads against a wall with all the insanity Satan has brought into our society. We need to turn back to God and in a hurry! All the world needs to lie prostrate before the Lord and cry out, "HELP US JESUS, HELP US JESUS, HELP US JESUS!"

Satan will keep you coupled with ignorance causing racism and sexism to remain prevalent throughout the world. He keeps people afraid of each other and uninterested in one another's background or culture. He holds mankind in the position of poverty and feeds their mind to accept it and be complacent with it.

He has directed men and women to make a career out of welfare. He imprisons our elderly by barring them in their homes. They are fearful of our children who do not respect their wisdom anymore. He invokes the spirit of jealousy and envy in our hearts when we see our brothers or sisters doing well. Satan entices us with gossip and vicious rumors that spread like wild fire. He changes our entire attitude from smart and respectful believers to silly and idiotic children. He develops a lackadaisical character in us when it comes to studying and doing God's word; about our spouses feeling, rearing our children, and being the best in our careers.

Yes, we need to be totally observant when it comes to the trickery of Satan and his plots. Remember that you are in a war and you're fighting on the front-line against the Adversary and his army. However, remain steadfast, for Matthew 13:49, 50 tell us, *"so shall it be at the end of the world: the angels shall come forth, and sever the wicked from among the just. And shall cast them into the furnace of fire: there shall be wailing and gnashing of teeth."*

My friend, we as Christians must be ready for the coming of Christ and be "just", in order not to face the flames of Hell.

We should be infuriated by their [Devil and demons] acts and how they ruin our lives. You may know someone who is incarcerated—guilty or innocent. For that, you should be outraged. Someone you know is addicted to drugs and/or alcohol and you see how it is dominating their lives and damaging others. Be offended at the atrocities Satan has plagued upon the lives of our brothers and sisters. Some mother's daughter is stricken with AIDS while some father's son is killed in a senseless robbery. We should be mad with rage at the insanity that abides in our homes, community, and nation.

I had a teacher once tell me that people don't get mad they get angry and dogs go mad. She also said, "never say you hate someone for the word is too strong. We should say we dislike an individual." Well, that is all fine and good for certain particulars. However, when it comes to Satan and his crooks, I am **MAD** [def. Angry, frantic] and I **HATE** [def. Intensely hostile aversion, to dislike strongly, unkind] him and the evil bondage he has on this world. Read what the book of Proverbs states in 8:13.

"The fear of the Lord is to hate evil: pride, and arrogancy, and the evil way, and the forward mouth, do I hate."

Satan does not love Christians or the world! So why should we have any good sentiments for him? I know that I am sick of him and the tragedies he causes. I am sick of hearing of our children dying of abuse. I am sick of seeing my brothers and sisters walking the streets with blood-shot eyes and intoxicated minds. He has stripped them of all of their masculine and feminine qualities. I am sick of hearing about the famine and disease in the world, while many of us throw out food and abuse the medical system. I am sick of hearing children curse their parents while controlling the house. I am sick of seeing adults afraid of their own children and refusing to discipline them. I am sick of seeing beautiful people end their marriages over foolishness. I am sick of seeing young girls, who are not through playing with Barbie dolls, pregnant by some boy because he has cute eyes. I am sick of young men who can control a basketball on the courts better than their own anatomy. I am sick of people running to the psychics in order to hear something good. TRUST GOD! I am sick of children murdering each other over gym shoes. I am sick of double-talking preachers and teachers who say they love the Lord but do not challenge evil. HELP US LORD!

Come on Saints. If God is your all-and-all stand up for righteousness and shun evil. The first clause of Psalms 97:10 states, "ye that love the Lord, hate evil:' Oh yes saints, you have the right to hate Satan and everything he stands for, including individuals or groups that are wicked and despise and hate God. We stand for God and His word alone, and nothing should ever come between you and the Lord. Psalms 139:20-22 tells us, *"for they speak against thee wickedly, and thine enemies take thy name in vain. Do not I hate them, O Lord, that hate thee? And am not I grieved with those that rise up against thee? I hate them with perfect hatred: I count them mine enemies"*.

"Lord, they are my enemies too! I detest those who do not reverence Your name."

So, what is God's purpose in allowing this buffoon to run rampant throughout the world and raise havoc on mankind?

Well, it's not because He gets a kick out of seeing us in pain and agony. God wants to see if we, as a nation of people, will be brothers and sisters toward one another. God wants us to show love one to the other. Satan has humanity seeing each other as the enemy, instead of humanity seeing Satan as that depravity. God's knowledge and purpose puzzles mankind. Satan wants us cornered with ambiguity but we shall believe the Lord's report.

Sinners who are trapped in the Devil's domain find themselves alone and bitter. So, in order to invalidate your happiness as a Christian they will dishonor your belief in God. To coin a phrase, misery loves company and sinners want to share that experience with anyone. Well, in order to avoid that, you as a believer in Christ, must set up safeguards and protect your fortress against the haters of God.

I must warn you the very enemy could be the individual in your home. Yes, wife it could be your husband and husband, it could be your wife. Parents, it could even be your own children and children could even be at war with one another. Satan doesn't care who he possesses or who he destroys. I cannot stress this enough: **SATAN DOES NOT LIKE YOU NEITHER DOES HE LOVE YOU!** When you are a believer in Christ and all His righteousness you are then inscribed on Satan's hit list and place under satanic surveillance.

Your foes will watch you very, very closely. Just to see if you are the Christian you claim you are. My friend let us recognize Satan's spirit and character through people. Listen to their conversations. Are they always talking negatively and maliciously? Are they gossiping and boasting? If so, recognize it for what it is…Satan. He tries to lure you into these types of conversation and feelings. Once he has you involved next you are trapped. Satan's movement upon you will happen so quickly. His darkness will surround you, swallow you up and consume you. Next, you're trying to bring yourself out of depression, self-pity, doubt, confusion, low or no self-esteem, worry, and illness. This could lead to physical and mental maladies and trigger thoughts and feelings of suicide. Satan hates the believer. He causes husbands and wives to fight over finances, house chores, sex, religion, child rearing and everything from the biggest to the smallest. His job is to keep confusion abounding in your home, place of employment, and place of recreation. He is the master Hell-raiser. He tears siblings apart who don't speak to this day. He tears families apart and they become abandoned and sometimes left homeless.

Satan relishes in our woes and misery. Satan is miserable so he wants us to join him, but there will be none of that, for we are victors and not victims of his downfall and wrath.

Satan's manifestations are being like him in the spirit of hate and jealousy; impatience and deep wavering faith in God. Secondly, your character and personality becomes vain and boastful in heart and spirit. You lack true courage in facing responsibility, standing against sin, discouragement, failure, and everything that causes failure in living an honest Christian life. Thirdly, Satan will keep you disillusioned and desensitized to spiritual vision. You will become vague in your mental faculties, intelligence, and carrying out Holy Bible instructions with regard to your personal life.

Also, you will not experience freedom from the works of the flesh. Without the liberating power of God you will face eternal damnation.

"For the wages of sin is death: but the gift of God is eternal life through Jesus Christ our Lord." Romans 6:23.

Finally, Satan will characterize you as being ignorant in your private life and ignorant in the divine will of God. Your life will never reflect a lifestyle of prayer and Christian living. So, why does God allow this buffoon to run rampant throughout society and the world? Well, for one obvious reason and a reason many believers and unbelievers don't understand is to build faith and character in the believer and confound the unbeliever. When we endure trials and tribulation, we are as gold placed in a furnace melted down and molded by the hand of God to His fashion. However, the joy is to know that through it all God is with you and has not, will not, and cannot abandon us.

"When you pass through the waters, I will be with you, and through the rivers, they will not overwhelm you. When you walk through the fire, you will not be burned or scorched, nor will the flame kindle upon you." (Isaiah 43:2 Amp. Bible).

No matter how hard it gets, how dark the night, and how painful the experience the Lord our God will <u>be with you.</u> He has an unbreakable connection to humanity in which we will only understand through His Spirit.

In order to receive the reward promised to the lovers of Christ resisting evil and temptation must be endured.

"Blessed is the man that endureth temptation: for when he is tried, he shall receive the crown of life, which the Lord hath promised to them that love him." (James 1:12 KJV).

The Lord promises to strengthen and build us up during our moment of despair and anguish. He wants us to rejoice in the victory that we will experience leaving the storms of our lives. God wants humanity to rely on Him and rest assured that He is in every concern of our lives.

"*Be well balance [temperate, sober of mind], be vigilant and cautious at all times; for that enemy of yours, the devil, roams around like a lion roaring [in fierce hunger], seeking someone to seize upon and devour. Withstand him; be firm in faith [against his onset – rooted, established, strong, immovable, and determined], knowing that the same [identical] sufferings are appointed to your brotherhood [the whole body of Christians] throughout the world. And after you have suffered a little while, the God of all grace [who imparts all blessings and favor]. Who has called you to His [own] eternal glory in Christ Jesus, will Himself complete and make you what you ought to be, establish and ground you securely, and strengthen, and settle you.*" (1 Peter 5:8-10 Amp. Bible).

Satan comes in our lives to knock us down and tries to capture our faith and spirit. He penetrates our minds with loneliness and depression and causes us to believe that we are alone in our tragedy. If we are not steadfast to our belief in Christ, Satan can consume us. Yet, Christians must understand that they are not alone in their sufferings. The entire body of Christ is at war with Satan and his demons. We all become wounded in one way or another but Satan too is bruised and beaten from our kept faith. After the suffering, God comes and restores us and places us back into His comforts.

Other supportive scripture to prove God is building great believers and doers of His word are 2 Peter 1:4-9 and Jude 20-24. Read theses at your leisure.

God not only saves us from our sufferings with Satan but also uses him to save us from ourselves. Mankind has a tendency to be boastful and full of themselves. Believing that every wonderful thing that happens in the world and to them is because of who they are. God has to humble mankind so he will not be lifted in pride as Satan himself has done. The Apostle Paul tells the Corinthians in his second letter to them about a thorn in his side to keep him humble.

"And lest I should be exalted above measure through the abundance of the revelations, there was given to me a thorn in the flesh, the messenger of Satan to buffet me, lest I should be exalted above measure." (2 Cor. 12:7).

God had shown Paul many great things and lifted him to great heights carnally and spiritually, however, in order for Paul not to get, "the big head" and to become that man he once was, God saw fit to use Satan to keep Paul humble.

God yet, wants to provide some type of struggle for man to endure that their overcoming may reward them. The book of 1 John 4:4-6 tells us of the power that is already in us through Jesus Christ:

"Ye are of God, little children, and have overcome them: because greater is He that is in you, than he that is in the world. They are of the world: therefore speak they of the world, and the world heareth them. We are of God: he that knoweth God

heareth us; he that is not of God heareth not us. Hereby know we the spirit of truth, and the spirit of error."

Even if Satan is used to humble Christians we still have power over his attacks. That power comes by knowing God and having an on-going relationship with Christ. Obeying God's word and hearing His Spirit of truth and wisdom will lead mankind onto the path of righteousness.

Oh, blessed is he that overcomes for he shall inherit all things. The book of Revelations clearly states this throughout. I want you to meditate and believe the promises of Christ.

Read the following scriptures at your leisure: Revelation 2:7, 11, 17, 26-28; 3:5, 12, 21.

Furthermore, God uses Satan to demonstrate His conquering power to mankind over Satan. An example of God showing His authority to man is found in the first chapter of the book of Job. As the book begins, we find Job is one of the wealthiest and most prosperous men on the face of the Earth. We learn that Job fears God and lives an upright life. In the first chapter we find God asking Satan about his whereabouts and Satan says he is looking for something or someone to devour. So, the Lord tells him about Job and Satan tells the Lord to take down the protective wall you have built around Job. The Lord allows this but prohibits Satan from destroying Job.

"*...[v.12] And the Lord said unto Satan, BEHOLD, ALL THAT HE HATH IS IN THY POWER: ONLY UPON*

HIMSELF PUT NOT FORTH THINE HAND. So Satan went forth from the presence of the Lord."

    God shows He is still in control and that Satan can only do what God permits him to do. Satan cannot bring financial and physical destruction upon us unless it is God's permissive will, and God will set the limits. So why do the righteous suffer? This question is raised after Job loses his family, his wealth, and his health. Soon after we find three friends of Job debating with him with regard to his tragedies. They insist his suffering is punishment for sin in his life. Yet, a fourth man, Elihu, tells Job he needs to humble himself and submit to God's will and allow the trials to purify his life. Furthermore, Job questioned God to learn about the sovereignty of God and his need to totally trust in the Lord. In the end, Job regains health, happiness, and prosperity well beyond his prior state.

    We fail to see the blessings of God in our lives. All we focus on is Satan stripping us of everything and we question God. "Why me?" God may answer, "Why not you?" we don't look at going through great tragedy as a blessing from God. We do not see down the darkened tunnel and find a ray of light and hope. All we can see is despair and anguish. It is beyond our ability to understand all of the "whys" behind all the suffering in the world.

    Yet, God sees a chance to get the glory through our act of faith and perseverance. Despite torment and trials, Job was steadfast in his belief in God. We as Christians today are not exempt from broken hearts or suffering but through it all we, as Job, can rest in the fact that God is fair, omnipotent, omniscient, and sovereign.

God is always proving Himself and His power over Satan's power. He wants man to believe in Him and trust Him entirely. Through the might of His power he shows His kindness and mercy.

"He did this that He might clearly demonstrate through the ages to come the immeasurable [limitless, surpassing] riches of His free grace [his unmerited favor] in [His] kindness and goodness of heart toward us in Christ Jesus" (Eph. 2:7 Amp. Bible).

Well, you may be thinking how does God permit Satan to do what he does and uses him to humble us? Yet, we are to be thankful of God's kindness? Yes, it is the mystery of God that complicates our understanding.

"[The purpose is] that through the church the complicated, many-sided wisdom of God in all its infinite variety and innumerable aspects might now be made known to the angelic rulers and authorities (principalities and powers) in the heavenly sphere." (Eph. 3:10 Amp. Bible).

Christ not only proves himself to all of mankind but to all heavenly and demonic rulers. These principalities are quick to know that Christ is King of kings and Lord of lords.

God will also use Satan to retrieve a long, lost, and loved sinner. He will cause Satan to afflict people to bring them to repentance. The evidence is shown in Job 33:14-30:

"...[v. 18] he holds him back from the pit [of destruction], and his life from perishing by the sword [of God's destructive

judgment]. [God's voice may be heard by man when] he is chastened with pain upon his bed and with continual strife in his bones or while all his bones are firmly set...[v. 24] Then [God] is gracious to him and says, deliver him from going down into the pit [of destruction]; I have found a ransom [a price of redemption, an atonement]!

[Then the man's] flesh shall be restored; it becomes fresher and more tender than a child's; he returns to the days of his youth. He prays to God, and He is favorable to him, so that he sees His face with joy; for [God] restores to him his righteousness [his uprightness and right standing with God — with its joys]. He looks upon other men or sings out to them, I have sinned and perverted that which was right, and it did not profit me, or He did not requite me [according to my iniquity]! [God] has redeemed my life from going down to the pit [of destruction], and my life shall see the light!...[v. 30] to bring back his life from the pit [of destruction], that he may be enlightened with the light of the living" (Amp. Bible).

We are free from the bondage of Satan and his disciples through Christ's redeeming power. Our savior is so gracious to us that it is beyond our understanding. Yet, thanks to our God for His "Amazing Grace" that forgives all of us from our sins.

God loves us so strongly that He will go to what seems to be extremes in order to gain our attention, lives, heart, mind, and soul. He wants us, He loves, and He cares for us. The word of God tells us we are to love the Lord entirely the same.

"Jesus said unto him, THOU SHALT LOVE THE LORD THY GOD WITH ALL THY HEART, AND WITH ALL THY

SOUL, AND WITH ALL THY MIND. THIS IS THE FIRST AND GREAT COMMANDMENT." *(Matthew 22:37-38).*

If we do not love the Lord in all these areas with all our strength, Satan can and, believe me, will overtake us: heart, mind, and soul. It will all belong to Satan and he will do to your life what he chooses. Satan only needs the slightest opening, not even bigger than the eye of a needle, to weave him into our lives.

Satan captures your heart by possessing those close to you. He will use them to tear at you with words, emotions, actions, and evil behavior. Satan will use your wife or husband to abuse, embarrass, antagonize, and strip you of any esteem you may have. He will shred at your heart through your children by causing them to become disobedient, cocky, rebellious, and venomous. He will make them alcohol and drug dependent. He will incarcerate them.

He will lead them into fornication and adulterous lifestyles. He will even kill them. Satan is trying to steal your heart from God.

When he steals your mind he confines it to a life of depression, worry, self-doubt, and mental illness. The Devil builds mirrors around you and speaks to your mind causing you to despise your physical features. "I'm too fat" or "I'm too skinny," will be the words Satan will have you saying. Not only will he have you honing in on your features but also make you believe you're the ugliest person on Earth. He leads you to believe people are talking about you and saying scandalous words about you. He torments you with bad thoughts, dreams, and visions. He plagues your thoughts with suicide. Satan then has your mind.

Once he steals these from you, Satan has placed your soul into slavery.

The reason God allows Satan to continue is to purge man of all possibility of falling. The book of Revelation chapter 21 tells us of a new Heaven and a new Earth and how there will be no more pain, sorrow, or crying.

"And God shall wipe away all tears from their eyes; and there shall be no more death, neither sorrow, nor crying, neither shall there be any more pain: for the former things are passed away…[v. 7] HE THAT OVERCOMETH SHALL INHERIT ALL THINGS: AND I WILL BE HIS GOD, AND HE SHALL BE MY SON." (REV. 21: 4, 7).

The Lord will sweep into the spirit of mankind with His Holy Spirit and cleanse all bitterness and pain. He will give man the strength he needs to overcome his past tragedies and remember them no more.

My friend, please, I beg you to begin to see Satan for who he is. Satan is mad at and jealous of man. Satan is working under a dastardly mindset: jealousy, envy, and arrogance. Man has a title that Satan [Lucifer] no longer holds. That title is the governorship or caretaker of all the Earth. God granted man with that dominion. Furthermore, man was created after the likeness and the image of God. Satan is not in that picture neither is he part of the plan.

Satan…You Punk!

God allowed man to name every animal and he also named his wife, Eve, woman. Satan did not have this privilege. So, do not fall under his spell of disbelief and become a heretic. The Devil wants man oblivious to his game and for mankind to go into wickedness without seeing the pleasure of God.

"For the god of this world has blinded the unbelievers' minds [that they should not discern the truth], preventing them from seeing the illuminating light of the Gospel of the glory of Christ [the Messiah], Who is the Image and Likeness of God." (2 Cor. 4:4).

When we become believers' in Christ and His glory we are totally aware of the Devil's tricks. We become empowered with the Spirit and He gives us wisdom.

God has blessed me with the opportunity to counsel and teach men who are stripping the demon of alcohol and drug addiction from their lives. These men constantly share their personal experiences with me and after I hear them and examine them, its amazing how they are all the same. Satan invites man into his web and it seems all new, exciting, and attractive to the natural person. However, it soon becomes the "same ole, same ole," to coin a phrase. Satan will put you in a revolving door that you cannot find your way out. These gentlemen would say how they noticed their addiction becoming regimented and senseless.

Satan would speak to them through their conscience and tell them to "go ahead and pay that electric bill next month and keep the money and buy yourself a rock," telling them they deserve it. He already knows that you are in the dark so why not have you sitting in the dark.

BULLETIN: BULLETIN: SATAN HATES YOU!

For that reason you should find it very difficult to serve and enjoy a relationship with him [Satan]. Many of these young men have found themselves involved in criminal activity, murder, sexual promiscuity, homosexual activity, bestiality, and domestic abuse.

Many of their marriages and relationships have ended because of their addiction. They steal from their children and many of their families have just given up on them. Yet, all of this is clear to them by now in hindsight. They see how Satan used them and made complete imbeciles of them. They describe it as being in a Bugs Bunny cartoon. The scene where Elmer Fudd is chasing Bugs Bunny off a cliff, yet, bugs Bunny stops and Elmer Fudd is left in mid-air. He then changes into a "sucker" or a "jack ass" before he falls. Yes, they feel very foolish and recognize that their manhood is robbed from them. However, the fact that they can take it back through the power of Jesus Christ is good news.

Our Lord and Savior will stamp a spirit of will power, courage, and discipline into your character so you will have the ability to take back what he steals from you.

"And if they are bound in fetters [of adversity] and held by cords of affliction. Then He shows to them [the true character of] their deeds and their transgressions, that they have acted arrogantly [with presumption and self-sufficiency]. He also opens their ears to instruction and discipline, and commands that they return from iniquity. If they obey and serve Him, they shall spend their days in prosperity and their years in pleasantness and joy." (Job 36:8-11 Amp. Bible).

Many people who have gone through great adversity have become intoned to the Spirit of God. All other responsibilities become secondary next to God. Christ shows man how everything took precedence to God and how man paid for that error. However, through obedience, joy and pleasure is given to man.

How is this achieved? Through repentance. The definition of repentance found in Webster's dictionary is – to grieve for sins committed or for things sinfully left undone – to feel extreme regret – to change one's mind and regret the original decision. Repentance is truly an act of the mind and heart. Your repentance must be extremely sincere and honest. You cannot have feelings vacillating or longings for the previous lifestyle. This prayer of repentance cannot be fraudulent or adulterated with lies and dishonesty. God knows the very recesses of our hearts and can weigh the good and evil intentions that are there.

"A GOOD MAN OUT OF THE GOOD TREASURE OF HIS HEART BRINGETH FORTH THAT WHICH IS GOOD; AND AN EVIL MAN OUT OF THE EVIL TREASURE OF HIS HEART BRINGETH FORTH THAT WHICH IS EVIL; FOR OF THE ABUNDANCE OF THE HEART HIS MOUTH SPEAKETH." (Lk. 6:45).

Our Lord is not unintelligent. He knows exactly what you are going to say before you say it. He knows if your prayer of repentance is real or if it is another game you are playing. So, do not mock God and begin to think in your mind you are forgiven. The feeling of not being forgiven will still burn in your heart and you will always question, "am I forgiven?" It will not happen until you are totally sincere.

People who have been in relationships know when someone is asking for true forgiveness or they are having their leg pulled. When you are serious you may show up with gifts, on one knee, and begging and crying. Now, the individual who is the recipient of all of this emotion weighs the sincerity of that person. So, if they are believed, they are then forgiven, but when it comes to God we do not express such emotion. Satan leads you to believe that any *"old prayer"* will do to satisfy God. I say, do not be deceived. Be passionate in your repentance to God and you will defeat the Devil.

You are now beginning to attack Satan and wage war on his compound. He knows the word of God is sown in your heart and Satan will soon come along to steal it.

The gospel according to St. Mark fourth chapter we find Jesus teaching a multitude a parable about a sower planting seeds. In this parable some of the seeds are eaten by birds, while some fell among the rocks where there was no soil and did not take root. Other seeds fell among thorns but the thorns choked their growth. Yet, some seeds fell on good ground and brought forth grain. So, in verses 15 through 19 Jesus tells us that the word of God falls into the hearts of men this very way:

Rev. Marvin L. Holden II

"THE ONES ALONG THE PATH ARE THOSE WHO HAVE THE WORD SOWN [in their hearts], BUT WHEN THEY HEAR, SATAN COMES AT ONCE AND [by force] TAKES AWAY THE MESSAGE WHICH IS SOWN IN THEM. AND IN THE SAME WAY THE ONES SOWN UPON STONY GROUND ARE THOSE WHO, WHEN THEY HEAR THE WORD, AT ONCE RECEIVE AND ACCEPT AND WELCOME IT WITH JOY; AND THEY HAVE NO REAL ROOT IN THEMSELVES, AND SO ENDURE FOR A LITTLE WHILE; THEN WHEN TROUBLE OR PERSECUTION ARISES ON ACCOUNT OF THE WORD, THEY IMMEDIATELY ARE OFFENDED [become displeased, indignant, resentful] AND THEY STUMBLE AND FALL AWAY. AND THE ONES SOWN AMONG THE THORNS ARE OTHERS WHO HEAR THE WORD; THEN THE CARES AND ANXIETIES OF THE WORLD AND DISTRACTIONS OF THE AGE, AND THE PLEASURE AND DELIGHT AND FALSE GLAMOUR AND DECEITFULNESS OF RICHES, AND THE CRAVING AND PASSIONATE DESIRE FOR OTHER THINGS CREEP IN AND CHOKE AND SURROCATE THE WORD, AND IT BECOMES FRUITLESS."

We must prepare ourselves to be good ground for the word of God to manifest in us. Once the word grows in us then the world [mankind] can see Christ in us. All of Heaven is rejoicing and all of Hell is groaning. You belong to Christ now and no devil in Hell can pluck you out of His hands. Yet, there is a job for us. We must remain in His word and vigilant in our conduct. Sure,

Satan will try you to see how serious you are and even if you are not, he can draw you back into his camp. Most people are ready when they are tired of being sick and tired. If not, you are only fooling yourself. You will find yourself in the revolving door of Satan again and doing the *"same ole, same ole"*. He'll keep you entertained with morbid foolishness and may promote you into profound deviltry.

"BUT WHEN THE UNCLEAN SPIRIT HAS GONE OUT OF A MAN, IT ROAMS THROUGH DRY [arid] PLACES IN SEARCH OF REST, BUT IT DOES NOT FIND ANY. THEN IT SAYS, I WILL GO BACK TO MY HOUSE FROM WHICH I CAME OUT. AND WHEN IT ARRIVES, IT FINDS THE PLACE UNOCCUPIED, [UN] SWEPT, NOT IN ORDER, AND [UN] DECORATED. THEN IT GOES AND BRINGS WITH IT SEVEN OTHER SPIRITS MORE WICKED THAN ITSELF, AND THEY GO IN AND MAKE THEIR HOME THERE.

AND THE LAST CONDITION OF THAT MAN BECOMES WORSE THAN THE FIRST. SO ALSO SHALL IT BE WITH THIS WICKED GENERATION." (MATT. 12:43-45 Amp. Bible).

That demonic spirit that once possessed your body and proved itself through some sinful nature, once cast out will try to return. When God's Holy Spirit comes into man, the Devil and his forces are no longer in control. However, you, the believer, have a duty to keep your temple [body] cleansed and separated [sanctified] from evil. Meaning, if you were an alcoholic you must remain removed from those enticements and people who will enable you to use again. If you were an adulterer you must remove yourself from those temptations and keep praying to God to keep idle thoughts of lured romances off your mind. If not, these demonic forces will come back to see if you are decorated with the Spirit of Christ. Also, when this demon returns, he will bring seven more worst than himself. You, my friend, if you are not serious in your repentance and your Christian way of life, wickedness will over power your life in its most corrupt fashion than you have ever experienced before.

Yes, your walk with Christ is serious because Satan is serious and he is playing a serious game. So, if you are a hypocrite and enjoy playing "church" and playing with the Spirit of God, you will pay.

"Be not deceived; god is not mocked: for whatsoever a man soweth, that shall he also reap." (Gal. 6:7).

In the letter to the Romans the first chapter at the 21st through the 32nd verses we read that God gives man up to his unrighteousness.

"Because that, when they knew God, they glorified Him not as God, neither were thankful; but became vain in their imaginations, and their foolish heart was darkened. [v. 22] Professing themselves to be wise, they became fools, [v. 23] and changed the glory of the incorruptible God into an image made like to corruptible man, and to birds, and four-footed beasts, and creeping things. [v. 24] Wherefore God also gave them up to

uncleanness through the lusts of their own hearts, to dishonor their own bodies between themselves.

[v. 25] Who changed the truth of God into a lie, and worshipped and served the creature more than the Creator, who is blessed forever, Amen. [v. 26] for this cause God gave them up unto vile affections: for even their women did change the natural use into that which is against nature: [v. 27] and likewise also the men, leaving the natural use of the woman, burned in their lust one toward another; men with men working that which is unseemly, and receiving in themselves that recompense of their error which was meet. [v. 28] And even as they did not like to retain God in their knowledge, God gave them over to a reprobate mind, to do those things which are not convenient; [v. 29] Being filled with all unrighteousness, fornication, wickedness, covetousness, maliciousness; full of envy, murder, debate, malignity; whisperers, [v. 30] Without understanding, covenant breakers, without natural affection, implacable, unmerciful: [v. 31] Who knowing the judgment of God, that they which commit such things are worthy of death, not only do the same, but have pleasure in them that do them."

Understand Satan takes that which God created and perverts it to his own satisfaction. Satan will have you going to church and associating with other Christians and even singing in the choir leading you to believe that that is all it takes to making it to the Kingdom of God. However, Satan will keep you in a sinful nature and whisper to you, "it's all right to do, you went to church". He will have you singing in the choir like a bird yet your heart is filled with hatred and filthiness. Yes, he will allow you to be a deacon yet your spirit is filled with debate and stealing the God-given authority from the pastor. He will even make a fool of the preacher. Having him believe it is okay to exhort the word of God and keep his fornication and adulterous acts ongoing. The entire church is fooled believing it only takes going to church to please God and He wants us to enjoy all the pleasures of life. To the natural eye that sin is cloaked in the "pleasures of life", but yet to the spiritual eye, sin is a one-way ticket to Hell. Satan is out to take the whole church to Hell and we are "fools" to believe any differently. So, we must put on the whole armor to fight back.

THE CHARGE OF THE SAINTS

When a Christian is born again he enters into the realm of the supernatural and spiritual; and he should begin a diligent study of the Holy Bible. Studying the proper way to walk and conduct himself in spiritual warfare with Satan and his demons.

You must be "suited and booted" like a knight in shining armor. You must be skilled in the use of your sword, able to sustain the weight of your breastplate, and strong enough to endure your shield. The book of Ephesians chapter six tells us we must brave the armor of God.

"[v. 11] Put on the whole armor of God, that ye may be able to stand against the wiles of the Devil. [v. 12] For we wrestle not against flesh and blood, but against principalities, against powers, against the rulers of the darkness of this world, against spiritual wickedness in high places. [v. 13] wherefore take unto you the whole armor of God, that ye may be able to withstand in the evil day, and having done all, to stand, [v. 14] Stand therefore, having your loins girt about with truth, and having on the breastplate of righteousness; [v. 15] And your feet shod with the preparation of the gospel of peace; [v. 16] Above all, taking the shield of faith, wherewith ye shall be able to quench all the fiery darts of the wicked. [v. 17] and take the helmet of salvation, and the sword of the Spirit, which is the word of God. [v. 18] Praying always with all prayer and supplication in the

Spirit, and watching thereunto with all perseverance and supplication for all saints."

Why is all of this necessary? Well, because, as stated earlier, Satan is after your heart, mind, and soul. If your head is protected with the helmet of salvation [from destruction/from sin or its consequences] he CANNOT penetrate your mind with perverted, idle, and suicidal thought. Wearing the breastplate of righteousness PREVENTS him from capturing your heart and taking you into depression, self-doubt, bitterness, hatred, cruelty, and mediocrity. Furthermore, the scripture tells us to girt our loins with the truth and shod our feet with the gospel of peace. If the believer stands with integrity and moral rectitude and be firmly-footed in righteousness, Satan will not have the power to lead you into a path of evil, fornication, adultery, homosexuality, murder, etc.

Many people are living their lives without the proper battle attire and wonder why they are in the position they are. By denying the word of God you open yourself to the attack of Satan and his allies. We see our society plagued by all kinds of turmoil and agony. We need to turn back to God and become sincere in our efforts. We need to go back to parenting our children instead of them parenting us.

We need to become active in their schooling, their friends, and their sexual feelings. Take action to combat Satan in every way. You have to be three steps ahead of him because, God forbid, you fall short he will catch up and overtake you and your household. My friend, pick up your shield of faith and carry your sword which is the word of God with pride and confidence. Protect your soul from all the ammunition that Satan <u>will</u> fire at you. No armed forces in the world will lead their troops out into a battle or war unarmed or wearing only half their uniform. If so, the conflict would be a blood bath and bodies injured and slain everywhere. God is trying to protect us if only we allow Him.

"God is our refuge and strength, a very present help in trouble." (Psalms 46:1). *"Trust in Him at all times; ye people, pour out your heart before Him: God is a refuge for us."* (Psalms 62:8).

God is our security when we are bruised and battered and have no where else to turn. He is there, right by our side to constantly attend to our every need. We seek protection in people, food, and material items but we soon realize those things do not do the job. Once we put our belief in the Lord it is then that we find sweet serenity that no foe can steal.

"He that dwelleth in the secret place of the most High shall abide under the shadow of the Almighty. I will say of the Lord, he is my refuge and my fortress: my God; in Him will I trust. Surely He shall deliver thee from the snare of the fowler, and from the noisome pestilence. He shall cover thee with His feathers, and under His wings shalt thou trust: His truth shall be thy shield and buckler. Thou shalt not be afraid for the terror by night; nor for the arrow that flieth by day; Nor for the pestilence that walketh in darkness; nor for the destruction that

wasteth at noonday…[v. 14] BECAUSE HE HATH SET HIS LOVE UPON ME, THEREFORE WILL I DELIVER HIM: I WILL SET HIM ON HIGH, BECAUSE HE HATH KNOWN MY NAME. HE SHALL CALL UPON ME, AND I WILL ANSWER HIM: I WILL BE WITH HIM IN TROUBLE; I WILL DELIVER HIM, AND HONOR HIM. WITH LONG LIFE WILL I SATISFY HIM, AND SHEW HIM MY SALVATION." *(Psalms 91:1-6, 14-16).*

See how much God wants to protect us from trouble, terror, fear, and destruction.

He will bring us out of Satan's dungeon of despair just because we have placed our love upon Him. God will honor us for our **SINCERE** love. Despite what society has fed us, God loves us. He loves us extremely and beyond anything we could understand. His love for us is profound, mysterious, scholarly, and intense. Nowhere can we find this type of love. Because man deals in the natural/flesh and God deals in the supernatural/spirit His love surpasses any and all our desires. God's love shatters the evil fetters that Satan has placed on us. God's love extracts the yoke that binds us to Satan's ungodliness. God is a power-source of love and truth and that confounds Satan. He will never understand the meaning and essence of God. Satan will remain in **AWE** of God because of His love and the love His people show in return. Satan is also resentful of mankind because He loves us so that He gave His only begotten Son for the world. Satan will be nothing like God. God is Holy, Majestic, Righteous, Strong, Great, Unique, and Eternal.

His many attributes are Faithful, Stable, Merciful, and Kind. Well, as for Satan he is everything that opposes God. Because you love God so, he will mask himself to be God. So, we must be cleaver of his tactics and give him no place to dwell.

"Neither give place to the devil. Let him that stole steal no more: but rather let him labor, working with his hands the thing which is good, that he may have to give to him that needeth. Let no corrupt communication proceed out of your mouth, but that which is good to the use of edifying, that it may minister grace unto the hearers. And grieve not the Holy Spirit of God, whereby ye are sealed unto the day of redemption. Let all bitterness, and wrath, and anger, and clamor, and evil speaking, be put away from you, with all malice: And be ye kind one to another, tenderhearted, forgiving one another, even as God for Christ's sake hath forgiven you." (Eph. 4:27-32).

We must take on those many attributes of God and use them in our daily lives. Let us not wear kindness only when we are seeking something from someone. Do not say kind things if it is only sarcasm. There is a saying that goes, "if you have nothing good to say, say nothing at all". Learn to be true to your friends, family, and people as a whole. When we use our words cruelly toward one another, God is grieved by our bitterness. He wants us to put those sinful deeds to death and awaken the love in our hearts. God's word is common sense and what could be more sensible than to treat people the way you would want to be treated.

Another device of Satan's is to make you believe that you are the only one going through great trials and tribulation. Yet, don't be tricked and hold fast to your faith in God and He will strengthen you. My friend, you are not alone in your afflictions. We, as a society, are all entangled in some problem or pain. No one is sailing through life and living comfortably on "Easy Street". Do not let Satan fool you with that one. The rich suffer just as the poor, and the healthy are just as ill as the sick.

"Withstand him; be firm in faith [against his onset — rooted, established, strong, immovable, and determined], knowing that the same [identical] sufferings are appointed to your brotherhood [the whole body of Christians] throughout the world" (1 Peter 5:9 Amp. Bible).

Yet, the glory in it all is that our Lord and Savior took on our sufferings and left them at the cross. We are not labored with those problems because Christ rose with victory over Death, Hell, and the Grave. My friend, go through your affliction in the faith of Jesus Christ, No Cross, No Crown.

We as Christians are all being attacked by Satan and going through some sort of trial or tribulation because we love God and want to dwell with Him. Do you remember the bulletin? **SATAN DOES NOT LOVE YOU, HE HATES YOU!!** Is that clear? He is out to steal your priceless soul. Remain sober and vigilant so you will not be devoured.

In the Gospel according to St. Matthew chapter four we find Jesus being tempted by the Devil. The Holy Spirit leads Jesus into the wilderness and He went without food for 40 days and nights. Satan tried to use Jesus' hunger to his advantage. The great tempter said to Him in verse three, *"if you are God's Son, command these stones to be made bread"*. Now, remember that Jesus has not eaten in 40 days and Satan tempts Him with the thought of turning stones into bread. Think how you would feel after 40 days of fasting then having thoughts of some warm-buttered bread haunting your mind. Yet, Jesus does what we should do now, overcome the Devil with the word of God.

"[v. 4]...IT IS WRITTEN, MAN SHALL NOT LIVE BY BREAD ALONE, BUT BY EVERY WORD THAT PROCEEDTH OUT OF THE MOUTH OF GOD." (Ref. Deut. 8:3).

Satan will come to you at your lowest point. When you feel empty and deprived he will offer you tantalizing treats to offset you from the gifts of God. Have you ever been at work on a fast and it seems that everyone is offering you something to eat? On no other day has someone offered you anything, but now they are ready to take you to lunch. He is at his best when you are at your least. He will use people, unknowingly, to work against you. [Remember the double reference in the beginning of the book]. However, remain steadfast in your purpose and God will pour out a blessing you deserve. Psalms chapter 37 and verse four tells us to *"Delight thyself also in the Lord; and He shall give thee the desires of thine heart"*. We can go without Satan's empty and temporal gifts when we serve a God who can supply us with an overwhelming abundance of everlasting blessings.

Rev. Marvin L. Holden II

Satan further tempted Jesus. He takes Jesus into the holy city [Jerusalem] and places Him on a pinnacle of the temple. He urges Jesus to cast Himself down and God will give Him charge of the angels that He will not hit the ground. Jesus again condemns him with the word of God.

"[v. 7]...THOU SHALT NOT TEMPT THE LORD THY GOD." *(Ref. Deut. 6:16).*

God has blessed many of us [Christians] with great paying jobs and positions in which we are receiving top salaries and loving our successful place on top of the ladder. If we allow Satan to convince us that these high positions and big dollars are the only particulars we need, we will surely take a plunge onto the rocks below. The love of money can bring down the sinner and the saint. Satan can take you down with the love of money [See 1 Tim. 6:10]. Do not allow material items to overtake you. These are creations, which Satan wants you to place before the Creator, in order that you might fail. Tell Satan to move out of your space. Be vocal and tell him he cannot tempt you. Treat him as if he were the neighborhood bully going around picking on everyone. Be bold and grab that little punk by his collar and tell him he will not bother you, your family or friends anymore. Pop Satan in his eye, kick him in his teeth and send him home crying. That punk!

The next verse is the clincher. Here Jesus is led into the high mountains and shown the kingdoms of the world and their glory. Satan then tells Jesus Christ, "**if** you bow down and worship me," he will give Christ what already belongs to Him. Yet, in Satan's own words there is question, doubt, and wavering. He is bold enough to go out on a limb, but too scared to command Jesus Christ to bow down. Why didn't he command Christ? Satan is a creation and he lacks the authority or the power to command the Creator to do anything. Satan is the instrument of God. He wants to lead us into his world in order that we worship him. Yet, what better way to capture all of humanity than to have our Lord and Savior surrender to him? Yet, in His power and in His might He commands Satan, "...[v. 10] GET THEE HENCE, SATAN: FOR IT IS WRITTEN, THOU SHALT WORSHIP THE LORD THY GOD AND HIM ONLY SHALT THOU SERVE".

Our Lord and Savior put this "punk" in his place and ordered him to move from Him and worship and serve God only. This coward has no more tricks up his sleeve or lame orders. So, he does what any worthless and chicken-hearted leader does. **LEAVES!**

Also, notice in the third and sixth verse of St. Matthew that Satan wants Jesus to prove His position as the Son of God. "If thou be the Son of God," then prove yourself. Satan does this identity check with Christians also. "Prove to me that you love God," Satan will say to you. You may begin thinking, "how do I love God?" then you will fall into debate with yourself over the fact that you love God. Once Satan has you debating that, he will question you, "if you are a Christian, how do you know and are you serving Him?" All of this questioning is suppose to cause you to waver in faith as he had hoped

Jesus would. However, Jesus fed Satan the word of God to rebuke him and we must do the same. Do not let Satan cause you to doubt your salvation!

Satan fails to understand that although he has great knowledge and vast experience in dealing with humanity, this knowledge and experience is acutely wee compared to God's intelligence and wisdom. Oh, how foolish and stupid he must feel knowing he cannot win. He is limited in his ability and his stronghold. He is neither omnipotent nor all-powerful. He is not omniscient, omnipresent, or even *"with it"*. Satan is not immutable. These qualities belong to God and God all by Himself. Our duty is to keep shoveling the word of God into Satan's filthy mouth.

He will loose his hold on you and run with fear from the pressure applied to him by the word of God. Satan does wrong, but we must do what is right in order to remain victorious over his grip.

"I write you, fathers, because you have come to know [recognize, be conscious of, and understand] Him Who [has existed] from the beginning. I write to you, young men, because you are strong and vigorous, and the word of God is [always] abiding in you [in your hearts], and you have been victorious over the wicked one." (1 John 2:14 Amp. Bible).

Reprove Satan with your testimony and encourage others who do not know Christ or those who are weak in spirit. Let them know that God is still answering prayer. Your testimony is a whip to Satan. He takes a lashing every time you open your mouth about the goodness of

God. Tell people of your amazing healing from cancer, heart disease, blindness, stroke, etc. Tell them God removed the despair and depression from your mind and the mental illness you were facing. Tell them of the great financial debt you were in until God opened up the doors of prosperity. Tell them how God has confounded the wise with His Majesty and has put Satan in his place. Tell them how God snatched the desire of drugs, alcohol, and cigarettes from your flesh. Exhort the Lord every chance you get and tell the devil he is a punk. Oh Satan, you have no hold here. We have overcome him by the blood of Jesus Christ and our testimony.

"And they have overcome [conquered] him by means of the blood of the Lamb and by the utterance of their testimony, for they did not love and cling to life even faced with death [holding their lives cheap till they had to die for their witnessing]." (Rev. 12:11 Amp. Bible).

Oh yes, I am excited! I am glad I know Jesus for myself and you should be jumping every time you hear the name of Jesus. Isn't it fascinating that the <u>name</u> of Jesus alone carries extremely major power? No other name under the heavens causes men and women to bow down. No other name makes devils run for their lives. No other name has majesty and honor.

I remember on one occasion speaking to a congregation of people at a church.

The Spirit of God led me to tell them all to say their names aloud. Soon a wave of soft-spoken murmuring went across the sanctuary. The parishioners looked at me as if to say, "what point is he trying to make?" Then the Spirit of God told me to tell the people to say, "Jesus." The congregation said, "Jesus," in a whisper. Yet, in a very brief moment, the whisper turned into a roar. The entire congregation began to howl the name, "Jesus," with a spirited passion. They soon began to stand to their feet and worship and praise the Lord. The praise seemed to go on forever. The Lord revealed to us that our names mean nothing. No matter how much we love our names and spend precious time choosing them, they mean nothing; yet the name of Jesus floods our very soul. The name of Jesus boils our emotions and reminds us of all the good and wonderful things He has done for us. My friend, there is POWER in the name of JESUS!

Saints, we share in the authority and power of our Lord and Savior. The Father exerted power in Christ when He raised The Anointed One from the grave and placed Him on His right side. So we as believers are above all rule and authority. We only answer to our Heavenly Father. Read about the power of Christ's name in Ephesians 1:19-22 and 2:6.

"And what is the exceeding greatness of his power to usward who believe, according to the working of his mighty power, which he wrought in Christ, when he raised him from the dead, and set him at his own right hand in the heavenly places, far above all principality, and power, and might and dominion, and every name that is named, not only in this world, but also in that which is to come: And hath put all things under his feet, and gave him to be the head over all things to the church."

[2:6] *"And hath raised us up together, and made us sit together in heavenly places in Christ Jesus."*

Never let your faith go. If you believe in Christ realize we will suffer the same trails and tribulations He suffered. Yes, we must go through the fire and through the flood, but we will not be absorbed [See Isaiah 43:1-2]. Never say, "why me Lord?" Learn to say, "Thank you Lord." Tell the Devil he is under your feet, never to rise again. Christ has already taken the keys of Death, Hell, and the Grave from Satan and next we are going to lock him up in his kingdom.

Notice first Corinthians 15:55 reads, "O death, where is thy sting? O grave, where is thy victory?" We will not suffer the sting of death and its agonizing blows nor will we comprehend its finalities and hopelessness. We will not give victory to the grave because it will not be able to contain us due to our Savior's powerful resurrection.

We, who are saved, are precious to God and are very delicate and fragile to Him. Because of our high price He handles us with special care.

"For we are the sweet fragrance of Christ [which exhales] unto God, [discernible alike] among those who are being saved and among those who are perishing." (2 Cor. 2:15).

Each one of us is a new sweet smelling flower belonging to God. He grooms us and tends to our needs so we won't choke from that deeply rooted weed...the Devil.

My friend, realize that you are more precious than gold to Christ. You are priceless, exquisite, unique, and the only individual with the God-given talent to do His task. You are the only one who can carry it out. You must be prepared to carry this great responsibility. You are a knight chosen by our Great King to go out into the kingdom and slay the oppressing dragon. Remember that you have the power of God within and He is protecting you. So, are you ready for the challenge? Will you answer when called upon? Are you courageous or fearful? Are you willing and waiting or doubting and incapable? Don't let Satan decide what job you're going to do for Christ. Satan will cause you to believe that you are on the team when in reality you are sitting in the sidelines…watching. Jesus tells us in Luke 9:62, "NO MAN, HAVING PUT HIS HAND TO THE PLOUGH, AND LOOKING BACK, IS FIT FOR THE KINGDOM OF GOD."

So, if there is no purpose or direction in your walk or service to Christ, you need to take an inventory of your life. You may be spending a great deal of time with Satan and servicing him. Ask yourself, "am I the bench-member in the church who does nothing in or outside of the church? Do I turn my back on people in need? Am I the minister who only wants to minister to great crowds on Sunday mornings?

Do I schedule when I am going to be a sinner and when I am going to be a saint?" Do you believe just paying your tithes and offering to the church will get you

Satan...You Punk!

into the kingdom of God? Has Satan lead you to believe that God can only make you feel better as you endure a fatal disease or do you believe God HEALS? My friend, you better check yourself! Unwavering faith in God is not acceptable or useful. God cannot use a cowardly soldier.

You may be cringing because one or more of the questions you asked yourself stepped on your feet. Now you are uncomfortable and uninterested in continuing to read. Well, that is the attitude Satan wants you to have. He wants you to be stubborn and bitter toward any change in your life that will better you. Satan may be telling you now, "Put this book down...what does he know? Hey, you are doing the best you can...what more does God want from you?" Well, know this. God expects the best from His servants. Sure, He knows we will fall short at times, but we should not believe that our shortcomings are our best. My Christian friend, believe you can overcome Satan and his demons. Overcome him by the birth of the Holy Spirit and with faith.

Jesus told His disciples of a promise to them and all humanity of a Comforter that is come which is the Holy Ghost (Jn. 14:26). Jesus tells them that the Comforter will teach them all things and bring those things He said back to their remembrance. Well, Christ has taught us the action we must use on him [Satan] in order to rid ourselves of him. We must receive the Holy Ghost to defeat the Devil. The Holy Ghost is the power over the rule of Satan. In the book of Acts of the Apostles, Christ, in His ascension to Heaven, tells that power is given to those who receive the Holy Ghost.

"BUT YE SHALL RECEIVE POWER, AFTER THAT THE HOLY GHOST IS COME UPON YOU:" (Acts 1:8).

Power for you to overcome drug and alcohol addiction, lying, stealing, killing, fornication, adultery, and homosexuality. Whatever demon possesses you, the power of the Holy Ghost can overtake any habit you have. I say to you, have faith in God and His power, and you will receive His righteousness.

"If ye know that he is righteous, ye know that every one that doeth righteousness is born of him." (1 John 2:29).

When you are born out of righteousness and of the Holy Spirit, you will live a sinless life. You will know sin to be a horrible taste in your mouth and you would not want to experience it again. No one wants to be trapped by Satan's darkness…twice. Yet, there are those who are locked in his revolving door of sin and sickness and enjoy it and fail to recognize yet. These sinners are the ones to whom we witness and for whom we pray for deliverance. For that reason, Satan attacks Christians, but God has put His seed in His people, which make us diligent.

"Whosoever is born of God doth not commit sin; for his seed remaineth in him: and he cannot sin, because he is born of God." (1 John 3:9).

Through the power of God, we, as Christians, are to show the world the love of God. We must display Christ-like living to those who are trapped in the ignorance of Satan. Satan has sinners living immoral and defiling themselves, but the Christian must help them restore their lives. We must defeat Satan on every hand by doing well, being well, and treating each other well. We must keep His commandment to love one another. By living as an example of Christ the sinner will know we are His disciples.

"A NEW COMMANDMENT I GIVE UNTO YOU, THAT YE LOVE ONE ANOTHER; AS I HAVE LOVED YOU, THAT YE ALSO LOVE ONE ANOTHER, BY THIS SHALL ALL MEN KNOW THAT YE ARE MY DISCIPLES, IF YE HAVE LOVE ONE TO ANOTHER." (John 13:34-35).

Showing love to each other is the testament of faith that we, as believers, demonstrate to the world. Having faith in God and clinging to His commandments will catapult you over all of your circumstances. Christians must be obedient to the word of God in order to see results in our lives.

"Whosoever believeth that Jesus is the Christ [The Anointed One] is born of God: and every one that loveth him that begat loveth him also that is begotten of him.

By this we know that we love the children of God, when we love God, that we keep his commandments: and his commandments are not grievous. For whatsoever is born of God overcometh the world: and this is the victory that overcometh the world, even our faith. (1 John 5:1-4)

God is love, and if we are born out of that love we must inherently bear witness of that love to the world. How else can we defeat the hate of Satan unless we pour out love onto everyone he holds captive? Now, faith is a hard instrument for some to grasp. Faith is a state of believing that something will be even when it's not. However, many people can have faith in many things in and around their lives, yet when it comes to God it is very difficult to have faith. Well, you may be saying, "I can believe in those things that are tangible in my life. Those things I can see and feel are the things I can believe in, but I have a problem with the abstract." That is understandable because we are people who operate in the physical through our five senses: touch, taste, smell, sight, and sound. However, we fail to realize that these senses give us the ability to acquire faith. Each sense gives us an experience that we can remember however painful or pleasant it may be. That experience is our tangible source on to which we should hold and believe God for more tangible evidence of Himself. Example: You have come through financial, marital, and personal problems, yet you never believed or kept faith in God to bring you through the problems, however they ended. Whether you believed or not, in God and His capability, He will still bless the unjust, as well as, the just. He is not a God who respects one person over another. Now, I am aware that without faith it is impossible to please God [Heb. 11:6], but that doesn't stop Him from being God and doing what He wants to do. These past experiences are the tangible points in your life where God is operating and building your faith. Yet, you fail to see them because you are looking for fireworks from God in order to get your attention. The fireworks are all the trials and tribulations through which He has brought you. God is saying to you,

Satan...You Punk!

"I brought you through all of your woes even when you did not realize or believe. I did it!" Those memories create your faith in God and cause you to overcome in the world. Remember my friend, you are the one who has been bruised and battered, neglected and rejected. Those are the concrete facts in your life that should plant you into a fountain of faith.

You will have the strength and knowledge to believe that no matter what the tragedy, God brought you out once before and He will do it again. Those are the words of the faithful overcomer.

Satan enjoys clouding the mind with disbelief and the, "I can do it on my own" thinking. Satan wants you to have faith in yourself while he leads you into mischief and self-glorification. No one can tell you anything or advise you on the simplest things because you "know it all". Your spirit will be stubborn and uncompromising, and you will find it very difficult to get along with many people. You are now isolated, bitter and ashamed to own up to the truth about yourself. That truth is you need Jesus Christ to give you direction and purpose. You need not a superficial confidence in yourself but a spiritual assurance in the power of God and how He will work through you. The false promise Satan gives will always leave an entranceway for him into your heart. Doubt is his doorway to you in order that he may always have his hands on you. However, when we are born out of God's spirit and receive His powerful faith, no Devil in Hell can touch us.

"We know that whosoever is born of God sinneth not; but he that is begotten of God keepeth himself, and that wicked one toucheth him not." (1 John 5:18).

Now that you have the God-given faith and are sure of the past experiences in your life as being God-given experiences, you are almost there. You have Satan pinned to the mat and now it is time to defeat and incarcerate him. How do you go about that? Well, through the power of the Holy Spirit, you must be endowed with the power on high. Satan started in a position where he had to answer to man and that upset him. He is not only jealous of man, but also fearful because man reminds him of God. Remember that we are creations in the image and likeness of Him so, this raises some jealousy and fear in Satan. So now, Satan fills with rage and finds away to penetrate humanity with trickery and deception. He has moved humanity from holiness to evil, from being filled with God to being filled with us. He also leads us away from total belief to disconcerting doubt. Man is now in a lackadaisical mode and content with this emotion.

God has to empower us with a spirit to overtake and command such a simpleton spirit to come out of us. Satan does not want people to repent, so we don't. He does not want us to have faith, so we don't. He definitely does not want us to have the Holy Spirit, so we don't seek God's Spirit.

Yet, my Christian brother and sister, do not be hoodwinked by this oaf and allow him to cheat you out of your glorious reward in sharing in the God experience. The experience God will shower upon those who love Him and keep His commandments will be the delivering factor in your life. God's power will coat the flesh and overtake it in a manner in which it will never control you again. You will have complete control over the will of the flesh. The desires of your body will not lead you into everlasting darkness again and have you associating with Satan and his demons once again. You are lifted into a place of explicit peace and righteousness. Your spirit will become mesmerized and filled with wonderment to why you waited so long for God's cleansing. Yes, you are new and your carnal nature is dead in spirit and in mind. Your thoughts are no longer longing for sinful pleasures but for the sweet freshness of life and its raptures. I say to you, crave to have the removal of condemnation off your life and the majesty of God's Holy Spirit to consume you. When Christians walk after Jesus Christ they turn down the ways of the flesh and follow the Spirit. For this reason, Christ left glory, clothed Himself in sin, and conquered sin and death to show that we have the ability to do the same.

"...That the righteousness of the law might be fulfilled in us, who walk not after the flesh, but after the Spirit. For they that are after the flesh do mind the things of the flesh; but they that are after the Spirit the things of the Spirit. For to be carnally minded is death; but to be spiritually minded is life and peace. Because the carnal mind is enmity against God: for it is not subject to the law of God, neither indeed can be. So then they that are in the flesh cannot please God. But ye are not in the

flesh, but in the Spirit, if so be that the Spirit of God dwell in you. Now if any man have not the Spirit of Christ, he is none of his. And if Christ be in you, the body is dead because of sin; but the Spirit is life because of righteousness. But if the Spirit of him that raised up Jesus from the dead dwell in you, he that raised up Christ from the dead shall also quicken your mortal bodies by his Spirit that dwelleth in you. Therefore, brethren, we are debtors, not to the flesh, to live after the flesh.

For if ye live after the flesh, ye shall die: but if ye through the Spirit do mortify the deeds of the body, ye shall live." (Romans 8:4-13).

Mankind cannot go on living in filth and expect to go to Heaven. The word of God says we will die and are already dead because of the life we live.

We must seek the things that will draw us closer to God and His Spirit in order that we may live eternally with Him. Coming to God and Him filling you with His Holiness doesn't happen overnight. The believer must experience some things in order to walk in the Spirit of God. He must, through, pain-staking trials and temperament, create the believer all over again. You must change and brake from former habits and conditions. God will show you the better side of life but He will bend you, twist you, and nearly break you until you see the light. Once that happens you will realize that you cannot live that type of sinful life again.

"This I say then, walk in the Spirit, and ye shall not fulfill the lust of the flesh. For the flesh lusteth against the Spirit, and the Spirit against the flesh; and these are contrary the one to the

Satan…You Punk!

other: so that ye cannot do the things that ye would. But if ye be led of the Spirit, ye are not under the law. [v. 22]…But the fruit of the Spirit is love, joy, peace, long-suffering, gentleness, goodness, faith, meekness, temperance: against such there is no law. And they that are Christ's have crucified the flesh with the affections and lusts. If we live in the Spirit, let us also walk in the Spirit. Let us not be desirous of vain glory, provoking one another, envying one another." (Gal. 5:16-18, 22-26).

Now, these traits don't come easily. Surely, if you have never been gentle or meek in the past, how can you be like that now? It takes God to work and remove the qualities that Satan has established in you. God is making a new creature out of you…one that may take some getting use to. My friend, remember you came to Jesus with a lot of mess, physically and spiritually. Now Christ has to go through those physical and spiritual areas and form them to His liking. When Christ begins this process of cleansing you, your life doesn't instantly get better, yet the battle **seems** to get worst. Your spirit is at war with the flesh because those old habits of yours are fighting so they aren't removed.

You begin to fight because it is hard for you to give up your old laundry: smoking, drinking, promiscuous sex, stealing, murder, hatred, etc. Then Satan begins talking with you saying, "you need to leave that Christ thing alone because its making your life more difficult than before." I say, don't give into that spirit because Satan wants to pin you back to that same old soiled mat you lied on once before.

Stay in the battle and defeat those desires, needs and cravings. You are bigger than any devil [habit] that you have. Show that Devil that he will never navigate your life again and that you are in control.

Stay in the battle because it is your life and soul about which we are concerned. Keep praying and believing you are better than before and walk after God's likeness. Be diligent in His word and do the works God tells your spirit to do. God will make His Spirit known to you because you were so familiar with Satan's ploys that nothing else mattered. Yet, God promised that His Spirit would pour out upon all flesh, giving them power and boldness to witness all over the world.

"But this is that which was spoken by the prophet Joel; AND IT SHALL COME TO PASS IN THE LAST DAYS, *saith God,* I WILL POUR OUT OF MY SPIRIT UPON ALL FLESH: AND YOUR SONS AND YOUR DAUGHTERS SHALL PROPHESY, AND YOUR YOUNG MEN SHALL SEE VISIONS, AND YOUR OLD MEN SHALL DREAM DREAMS: AND ON MY SERVANTS AND ON MY HANDMAIDENS I WILL POUR OUT IN THOSE DAYS OF MY SPIRIT; AND THEY SHALL PROPHESY: AND I WILL SHEW WONDERS IN HEAVEN ABOVE, AND SIGNS IN THE EARTH BENEATH; BLOOD, AND FIRE, AND VAPOUR OF SMOKE: THE SUN SHALL BE TURNED INTO DARKNESS, AND THE MOON INTO BLOOD, BEFORE THAT GREAT AND NOTABLE DAY OF THE LORD COME: AND IT SHALL COME TO PASS,

THAT WHOSOEVER SHALL CALL ON THE NAME OF THE LORD SHALL BE SAVED." (Acts 2:16-21).

The name of the Lord is our safeguard and He saves us from any terror that Satan attempts to throw. The Holy Spirit is the covering Christians need when turning their lives over to Christ, even those who have backslid. Satan turns on his "punkish" attitude even greater and is angrier because he lost a soul to God.

He pulls out every tactic against you and brings back those familiar habits you once loved. When those desires hit you, my friend, begin to pray like you never prayed before. Ask God to increase your strength, cast out all former passions, and yield not to new ones. Be sincere and God will move quickly to your defense, because He knows the great challenges you face and how they can overwhelm you.

"...BE NOT AFRAID NOR DISMAYED BY REASON OF THIS GREAT MULTITUDE; FOR THE BATTLE IS NOT YOURS, BUT GOD'S." (2 Chr. 20:15).

We cannot fight Satan physically as if it were some street fight. He attacks humanity through his spirit and corrupts us physically. So, believers in Christ must garb themselves with God's Spirit to counter-attack Satan spiritually. Basically, it's a "spiritual thing" and mankind needs to let loose their selfishness and give this war back to God and His alliances that fought Satan and his forces. Satan has been fighting for dominance long before mankind; however, humanity has only heightened this battle for Satan. He sees it as an opportunity to gain even more allies to destroy God and His Kingdom. Yet, as long as we stand against Satan and serve God this will never happen nor will Satan even come close.

"...AND UPON THIS ROCK I WILL BUILD MY CHURCH; AND THE GATES OF HELL SHALL NOT PREVAIL AGAINST IT." (Mt. 16:18).

The Christian is the body or the church of Christ and once we have His Spirit surrounding us, Satan will not come near us. So, how do you achieve this mighty Spirit of God? It's simple. Ask. Be faithful and pray to God for His completeness and you will receive His passionate gift, one that will overtake you and fill you with clean, fresh, and Spirited-water. You will overflow in love, joy, and abundant gladness.

"HE THAT BELIEVETH ON ME, AS THE SCRIPTURE HATH SAID, OUT OF HIS BELLY SHALL FLOW RIVERS OF LIVING WATER." (Jn. 7:38).

The Spirit of God will have resonating, thunderous, and explosive geysers bursting from you. These fresh, cool, and vibrant fountains will flow from the abyss of your soul and you will birth a new spirit of unequivocal vitality.

You now have power to defeat Satan and bring him to his final doom. My friend, it is time to shut him down and put him out of the business of misery.

LOCK HIM UP AND THROW AWAY THE KEY

Sometime ago, being a member of a local church, there was a co-member there who had a very interesting flair and introduction to his testimonies. He would stand and yell at the top of his lungs, as if he were taunting the Devil, and say, "ain't nobody mad but the Devil and if you are a devil then you have a natural cause to be mad." I laugh every time I hear it because I can visualize Satan's insanity over losing the battle. However, the sad irony of this statement is that Satan's madness has infected a population of people and has driven them into exasperation.

The Devil's wrath comes from his own doing. He is aimlessly fighting a battle he will never win and by working on something so intensely as this he is driving himself crazy. Now, don't feel sorry for this fool, feel sorry for the ones on whom he is taking out his anger. He is definitely on a rampage and we, as a society, are his victims. He is out of control and needs policing. As every law-governing country in the world locks up people who are a menace to society, so does God. Now is the time to end Satan's run and personally take hold of him.

Spiritually, you can incarcerate Satan by doing the practices previously stated.

Rid him out of your life forever and entrap him with the Spirit of Holiness. Yes, lock up this mad man and remove the paranoia from your mind and in your home.

Yes, my brother and sister you need to repent and come to God. Don't let this opportunity pass and the sun go down on you.

Physically, God will have Satan bound and locked away to never torment again.

"And I saw an angel come down from heaven, having the key of the bottomless pit and a great chain in his hand.

And he laid hold on the dragon, that old serpent, which is the Devil, and Satan, and bound him a thousand years. And cast him into the bottomless pit, and shut him up, and set a seal upon him, that he should deceive the nations no more, till the thousand years should be fulfilled: and after that he must be loosed a little season." (Rev. 20:1-3).

If you remember when Satan then Lucifer tried to raise his throne above God's, an angel named Michael took care of that problem. Here we see an angel; again, doing his job and that is to react against evil.

Our Lord and Savior doesn't have to lift a finger to deal with such foolishness. He is too Holy to be in the presence of evil. So, we find this angel with the key to the bottomless pit, which is a perfect contrast to Satan...empty and bottomless. Also, a "great chain" is carried by the angel meaning the Devil must be of some great size and having uncontrollable madness. Not only is his prison locked up but it is sealed also to assure no escape. Yet, why is he only sentenced to 1,000 years and then released? Satan is given parole? Why serve a God who is going to let this maniac back out into society to torment us again? I'm sure you are asking those questions and "yes," there is an answer. Satan and his "punkettes" will go throughout the Earth to deceive the nations who refused Christ. Also, his purpose is to retrieve those individuals who, in their hearts, have longed for an opportunity to fulfill their lusts and to get rid of what they believe to be strict laws and rigid suppression.

"And when the thousand years are expired, Satan shall be loosed out of his prison. And shall go out to deceive the nations, which are in the four quarters of the earth, Gog and Magog, to gather them, together to battle: the number of whom is as the sand of the sea." (Rev. 20: 7,8).

Here is Satan's post-Millennium career to mobilize the rebels in the land of Gog and Magog, this is north of Palestine and Asia and he will ascend upon Jerusalem from the north. Gog is a symbolic name, representing the leader of the world powers antagonistic to God. This reference is also found in Ezekiel chapters, 38 and 39 which refers to an event pre-Millennium.

Therefore the Gog of Ezekiel is viewed as the head of the high regions northwest of Asia believed by some to be Russia. Remember that the book of Revelation is very spiritual and foretelling. Meaning, it has the double-reference of the natural: meaning the world will see this event take place and the spiritual: meaning it will happen in the supernatural for the glorification of God. The scripture goes on to tell that the rebels from all parts of the Earth will surround the camp of the saints and the capital, Jerusalem. Fire will come down from God out of heaven and devour every rebel [v.9]. It is now time for the punk, who has been bullying and terrorizing everyone, to be cast away forever and never seen again. This is our victory saint! This hoodlum has now been taken down. He is right where he belongs…under our feet.

"And the devil that deceived them was cast into the lake of fire and brimstone, where the beast and the false prophet are, and shall be tormented day and night for ever and ever." (Rev. 20:10).

Yes, all evil is gone and there is no more madness and insanity in the world. Our God has created a new Heaven, a new Earth, and a New Jerusalem and we are apart of the holy city. We will know those experiences no more and all regret is gone.

"And God shall wipe away all tears from their eyes; and there shall be no more death, neither sorrow, nor crying, neither shall there be any more pain: for the former things are passed away." (Rev. 21:4).

There will be nothing but joy, wonderful joy. Now, I ask you who's mad now? "Ain't nobody mad but the Devil." As I say, I laugh when hearing this statement, however, I can truly laugh with sheer pleasure now. I laugh at this scatterbrain. I laugh at your defeat. I laugh at your jealousy. I laugh at your failed attempts. I laugh at your mishandling of God's Earth. I laugh at your failed plot to rule the heavens. I laugh at your reckless stooges called demons. I laugh at your whole foolish kingdom and those who followed you. I laugh at you Satan…**You Punk!**

End

ABOUT THE AUTHOR

Rev. Marvin L. Holden II has been a licensed and ordained minister of fourteen years and spiritual speaker and teacher of the work of God. He has worked with men who have been trapped by the snares of drug and domestic abuse, homelessness and violence through a Christian mentoring program for the last eight years. *Satan…You Punk!* was inspired by God through Rev. Holden's personal battle with Sickle Cell Anemia and kidney failure in his life. He shares his story of how he received a kidney transplant donated by his wife and thereby the subject of an article in *Ebony* magazine. Rev. Holden teaches how to battle the machinations of evil through Holy living. How he combated against suicidal depression and illness. Through this supernaturally inspired text you will learn what God expects of you and how to attain those "holy" attributes in God. You will learn the ploys and tactics that Satan conditions an individual to hold on to and make excuses for. If you ever wanted to learn how to resist and discover the secret of his trade, then you need to read *Satan…You Punk!* Finally you will see the Devil for who he truly is, a punk.

Rev. Holden holds a degree in Communications and Professional writing and works as a coordinator for an organ procurement organization promoting and educating the public of the need for organ and tissue donation.

Printed in the United States
4877